Contents

Introduction

Innovations, first published in 2000, was created to provide intermediate to high-intermediate students with interesting models of natural spoken English to motivate them beyond the intermediate plateau. *Innovations* has now been updated and expanded into a new series (*pre-intermediate, intermediate, upper-intermediate*) for classes looking for a fresh approach. It is based on a language-rich, lexical/grammatical syllabus that starts with the kinds of natural conversations that learners want to have.

What's so innovative about *Innovations*?

Innovations intermediate, like the rest of the *Innovations* series, sets out to maximise students' ability to speak English fluently and to be able to understand natural spoken English. It does this not simply by providing students with plenty of opportunities to use language in personal, creative and communicative contexts, but more importantly, by providing a predominantly spoken model of English. The English presented in the whole *Innovations* series is the English commonly used in everyday life by native speakers. The series syllabus is designed to meet students' communicative needs. At all levels, the prime concern is what students will be able to *say* afterwards. As a result, the starting point for our syllabus is not the usual list of tense-based structures, but rather the typical kinds of conversations we believe students want to be able to have in English. What is then presented and practised is the language (both vocabulary and grammar) that will enable them to have those conversations.

How does *Innovations intermediate* fit in with the rest of the series?

Innovations intermediate aims to provide a large boost in language acquisition, which we feel is important at the intermediate level. It focuses on basic topic conversations and functions. Grammar tends to be presented either as fixed chunks of lexis to be learnt, or fairly short grammar sections which practise grammar in a fairly narrow context. Students are shown how to make the most of a limited vocabulary. *Innovations intermediate* presents more sophisticated versions of some basic conversations. It does this by presenting a wider range of responses to typical questions and by introducing some idiomatic language. It also covers a wider range of issues than *Innovations pre-intermediate* both through the reading texts and the choice of topics. Consequently, there is a greater vocabulary load. Grammar is now focused on more deeply through examples showing how it is used in different ways and in wider contexts. Tenses are contrasted more, meaning is discussed, and more 'difficult' structures such as conditionals are introduced. In *Innovations upper-intermediate*, the language is more idiomatic and focuses on more aspects of spoken grammar that are often neglected.

Organisation

Innovations intermediate is divided into twenty units. Each unit is further divided into three two-page sections, all of which provide self-contained and coherent lessons of 60–90 minutes, although obviously you may wish to alter these to suit your needs. All the units in *Innovations intermediate* contain at least one two-page section based on reading or listening. These sections, **Reading** or **Listening**, typically follow a pattern of pre-text speaking, a clear task for students to do while they read or listen, and speaking tasks and language work. Short reading texts and listening tasks are sometimes used elsewhere in the Coursebook to present language.

The other two two-page sections of each unit are **Using vocabulary** and **Using grammar**. These sections contain frequent speaking activities and aim to provide lots of examples of how vocabulary and grammar are actually used. Many of the exercises are in the form of short dialogues and are on the audio recordings, providing further pronunciation practice and developing listening skills.

There is a **Review** after every four units.

*   The **Tapescript** at the back of the Coursebook features all of the dialogues, with the missing words and phrases highlighted in colour for easier identification.

*   The **Grammar commentary** at the back of the Coursebook provides notes on the grammar presented in the course.

*   The **Expression organiser** at the back of the Coursebook allows students to record and translate some of the most important expressions in each unit.

Writing is not focused on in the Coursebook. However, there are thorough writing sections in all the odd units of the Workbook. These provide models of typical texts students are expected to write in exams such as PET and FCE. They are often followed by a short exercise on useful language for writing, and a writing task. The writing task often requires students to write a similar text to the one in the model.

teacher's book
Innovations

a course in natural English

Hugh Dellar and Andrew Walkley

with Richard Moore

United Kingdom • United States • Australia • Canada • Mexico • Singapore • Spain

Innovations Intermediate
Teacher's Book
Second Edition
Dellar/Walkley/Moore

Publisher: *Christopher Wenger*
Series Editor: *Jimmie Hill*
Editorial Manager: *Howard Middle/HM ELT Services*
Director of Marketing, ESL/ELT: *Amy Mabley*
Director of Development, ESL/ELT: *Anita Raducanu*
Developmental Editor: *Paul MacIntyre*
Editorial Assistant: *Christine Galvin*
Sr. Production Editor: *Sally Cogliano*

Associate Marketing Manager: *Laura Needham*
Sr. Print Buyer: *Mary Beth Hennebury*
Compositor: *Process ELT (www.process-elt.com)*
Production Management: *Process ELT*
Copyeditor: *Process ELT*
Cover/Text Designer: *Studio Image & Photographic Art*
(www.studio-image.com)

Printer: *Webcom*

Printed in Canada.
3 4 5 6 7 8 9 10 08 07

For more information contact Thomson Learning, High Holborn House, 50/51 Bedford Row, London WC1R 4LR United Kingdom or Heinle, 25 Thomson Place, Boston, MA 02210 USA. You can visit our Web site at elt.thomson.com

For permission to use material from this text or product, submit a request online at:
www.thomsonrights.com

ISBN-13: 978-0-7593-9843-6
ISBN-10: 0-7593-9843-7
Teacher's Book

Other components

The Coursebook is complemented by a set of two Audio CDs/Audio Tapes, a Workbook, this Teacher's Book, and a separate, photocopiable Teacher's Resource Book. There is also support in the form of a website with useful links, and the test-creating programme ExamView® Pro.

- **Audio CDs/Audio Tapes**
  The Audio CDs/Audio Tapes contain recordings of all the dialogues and reading texts, pronunciation exercises and those lexical exercises where stress and intonation are the main focus.

- **Workbook**
  The Workbook is for self-study, but any of the exercises in it may be done either in class or as homework. In addition, the Workbook contains writing tasks. Some of the Workbook exercises are directly related to activities in the Coursebook, making them useful for setting as homework, while others are more loosely connected and are designed to extend and expand students' knowledge of the language. If you choose not to use the Workbook in class, it is a good idea to recommend it to students as additional practice.

- **Teacher's Resource Book**
  The Teacher's Resource Book provides forty photocopiable activities and games which closely support the material in the Coursebook.

Getting the most out of *Innovations*

This Teacher's Book provides plenty of detailed advice on how to get the most out of *Innovations intermediate*. However, there are some general points to make about the special features you will find in *Innovations intermediate Coursebook*. These features are highlighted in the section that follows.

Features of Innovations

Using vocabulary

Each unit has a two-page section explicitly dealing with vocabulary. The tasks in these sections focus on the words, collocations and expressions students need in order to have common conversations on the topic of the unit. Exercises often explore the variety of typical responses to common questions like 'What's it like round there?' or 'How was your journey?', which then lead into personalised practice. Other exercises encourage students to have longer conversations or provide the kind of language they need to take longer turns. Because most of the vocabulary in these sections is in the context of its typical usage, the exercises often reveal common grammatical patterns, which you can draw students' attention to. As you go through the answers, you can also get students to repeat the key expressions, which provides them with practice in pronunciation. Many of the exercises are on the audio recordings. Finally, you can ask the kinds of questions mentioned in the section below, **Noticing surrounding language.** The notes in the Teacher's Book will help you with this.

Using grammar

Each unit contains a two-page section dealing with particular areas of grammar which spring naturally from the texts or which are central to the topic. All the main tense-based structures you would expect to cover at the intermediate level are here. Students consolidate what they have learnt earlier in the *Innovations* series. For example, whereas the **Using grammar** sections in *Innovations pre-intermediate* look at single uses of tenses and modals, in *Innovations intermediate* they look at several different uses and frequently contrast them with other structures and the way they are used. Again, the focus on typical usage often leads to practice with a dialogue or role play.

Apart from the traditional tenses, we look at some grammatical areas that are sometimes neglected, such as *get used to*, opinions with *must*, and verbs to talk about the future. In all the **Using grammar** sections there are also opportunities to focus on new vocabulary by getting students to notice the surrounding language. Attention is often drawn to typical vocabulary that goes with the grammar through the grammatical explanations and **Real English** notes. There are plenty of speaking tasks linked to the particular structure. Reference is always made to the corresponding section in the **Grammar commentary** at the back of the Coursebook.

Noticing surrounding language

Although grammar exercises are provided primarily to focus on particular structures, we have presented all such language in natural contexts. This means that the surrounding language is just as important as the language being more explicitly focused on. If the exercise concerns the present perfect, do not miss the opportunity to point out other surrounding common phrases and expressions at the same time. One of the most important ways students will improve on their own is if they notice more. Turn 'noticing' into a major classroom activity. In order to do this, you need to not only explain meaning, but also ask students questions such as:

What other things can you ... ?

What other things can you describe as ... ?

What's the opposite of ... ?

What's the positive/negative way of saying ... ?

If you do ... , what would you do next/what happened before?

Where would you ... ?

What do you use a ... for?

What would you reply if someone said ... ?

The aim of these questions is to generate useful language connected to the word or expression in the exercise and also for students to get an idea of the limits of collocations and differences with their own first language. Asking questions like these are better than simply explaining, for three reasons. Firstly, they allow you to check whether students have understood what you explained. Secondly, they are more engaging for the students as you are involving them in the teaching process and accessing their current knowledge. Thirdly, they provide opportunities to extend their knowledge by introducing new language. In some ways, the questions are also convenient for you as a teacher, because students provide meanings in attempting answers and you can then provide the actual language by correcting any mistakes or re-stating what they said in more natural English. This new language can also be put on the board, ideally in the form of whole expressions as you would use them in speech.

You may also like to follow up a section of teaching like this by asking students to briefly personalise any new vocabulary you put on the board. For example, you could ask:

Do you know or have you heard about anyone who ... ?

Do you know or have you heard about anyone who has ... ?

When's the last time you ... ? Where? What happened?

Can you use any of these words/phrases/expressions to describe things in your life?

Which is the most useful word/phrase/expression?

Which words/phrases/expressions do you like most?

You could put students into pairs to do this kind of exercise for five or ten minutes. This is a good way of breaking up the lesson and getting away from the Coursebook for a moment. It also encourages students to get to know each other better and, unlike supplementary materials, requires little planning and no fighting with the photocopier!

The teachers' notes often suggest questions you can ask about language in the texts and there are also good examples of these kinds of questions in the **Vocabulary quizzes** in the **Review** units. It may take a little time to get used to this style of teaching, and students also may initially need to get used to it, but it is worth persisting with it, as it produces a dynamic and language-rich classroom.

Grammar commentary

The **Grammar commentary** starts on page 160 of the Coursebook after a two-page introduction outlining the basic approach to grammar taken in the book. Ask students to read these pages early on in the course and discuss any questions that arise from it. The grammar points that follow refer to the **Using grammar** sections within the units. Generally, you can ask students to read the **Grammar commentary** as a way to review the language after they have looked at particular structures. However, in some cases you might want students to come up with a guideline or 'rule' themselves and then compare it to the explanation in the **Grammar commentary** before working on the exercises. The **Grammar commentary** is also another good source of useful examples for students to record.

Dialogues

Almost without exception, the listening texts are conversations. They contain the topics people talk about every day, and contain many commonly-used phrases and expressions. Many of these common expressions are re-cycled in the Coursebook.

Listening texts often occur at the beginning of a unit. This is because a lot of the language in the text is focused on in the rest of the unit. When you do these listening tasks in class, play the recording once so students can answer the gist questions in **While you listen** and then once more to allow them to identify the words and phrases which complete the gaps. If your students find this hard, play the recording a third time and pause after each gap to give them more time to write. Finally, play the recording one last time as students read the dialogue. Listening to natural spoken English whilst also reading what they are hearing helps students get used to the way language is 'chunked': where speakers pause, and more importantly, where they do not pause. It also helps them notice other features of everyday speech, such as discourse markers. You could follow up by getting students to read the dialogue aloud in pairs – either the whole dialogue or just part of it. The other listening texts in the book are treated like more traditional skills lessons. However, if you and your students like the gap-filling activities, you could copy the relevant tapescript at the back of the book and blank out the expressions you would most like to focus on. Alternatively, pick out some key nouns or verbs.

Reading texts

Thirteen of the units in *Innovations intermediate* have two-page reading sections. These texts are derived from authentic articles, but have been re-written to include maximally useful vocabulary and collocations. The texts are all designed to elicit some kind of personal response from students, whether it be laughter, disbelief, or shock!

Encourage students to read the whole text through without worrying too much about any words they don't know. Tell them to put their pens down for a minute and relax! One good way of ensuring they do this is to play the recording as they read it the first time or, if you want a slower pace, to read it out yourself. Important vocabulary is focused on later, and students need to gain confidence in their ability to understand most – if not all – of a text. Encourage students to focus on the many words they do know!

Each reading text is followed by a speaking task where students have the opportunity to react personally to the text and to extend the discussion on a related theme. These tasks can either be done in pairs or in small groups. You may want to add some of your own questions connected to the text which you think will interest your particular class.

There are also often comprehension and vocabulary tasks that encourage students to re-read the text and notice useful expressions and collocations. One question that you can ask is if anyone found an expression or collocation that was interesting or new to them. For example, in **The day that changed my life** on page 26, students might find *I just did it on impulse* an interesting new expression. Suggest that students use a good English–English dictionary, not only to check the meaning of words but also to read the examples, which often contain useful collocations and phrases.

With both the reading and the listening texts, you could simply ask students *Do you have any questions about the text?* Note that this a different question to *Are there any words which you don't know?*, because it allows students to ask about anything. They can ask about words they *do* know, but which may appear in a new meaning or collocation; they can ask about expressions; they can ask about content; they can even ask you what *you* think!

Encouraging students to ask questions is a good way to encourage them to notice language. It also helps to create a good relationship between students and teacher.

Extra texts

Occasionally, there are smaller listening and reading texts such as **Two uses of the present continuous** on page 30 and **A good job?** on page 38. These are warm-up exercises that function as talking points at the beginning of the lesson. They provide short, natural contexts for the grammar that is focused on in the lesson.

Speaking

Speaking is an essential part of every lesson. The speaking tasks throughout the Coursebook are intended to encourage students to use some of the new language they have met in personalised ways. They are also an opportunity for students to relax and enjoy talking to each other! Whenever possible, introduce these speaking tasks by talking about yourself and encouraging the class to ask you questions. This serves as a source of language input as well as a model that students may follow. Also, students generally like finding out more about their teachers.

You may wish to use these discussion periods to monitor students' spoken performance and to gather student errors to focus on later, or to listen out for gaps in students' vocabularies which can later be addressed. A good way to give feedback on these sections is to re-tell what one or two students said. Re-telling what students say – sometimes called re-formulation – is a good technique because it allows even the weakest students to share their experiences and ideas with the whole class without the pressure of performing in front of them. It's quicker – there are no painful pauses – and it maintains the pace of the lesson. Finally, it allows you to correct and introduce useful new language in a way which acknowledges that the student has successfully conveyed their meaning. You can write some of this new language on the board, if you like, but it's not entirely necessary. Sometimes you may wish to just take a back seat and have no feedback.

Pronunciation

As *Innovations* places such an emphasis on spoken English, pronunciation is given a high priority throughout. The recording provides models of many short dialogues, language patterns and expressions. The recording can be used to help students practise the expressions. They should be encouraged to repeat the expressions several times chorally and individually until they can say them naturally. It is important that students do not just learn forms and meanings, but also learn how whole phrases and expressions are said by fluent speakers.

Real English notes

There are Real English notes throughout the Coursebook. These notes refer to a particular piece of language – word, phrase or grammatical structure – that appears in one of the tasks. The notes contain features of everyday English which many traditional coursebooks overlook, and so it is important to draw students' attention to the explanations and examples. Add more examples or ask a few related questions to exploit the notes further.

Review units

There is a **Review** after every four units. This gives students the chance to revisit and consolidate language they have studied. These **Reviews** have been written to use in class time and have a number of speaking activities. However, you may want to set some of the exercises as homework before the class. Two of these exercises are **Look back and check** and **What can you remember?**, where students recall information they have learned and repeat previous activities. Repeating activities, perhaps unsurprisingly, often leads to better student performance the second time round. You may want to have students do these exercises more regularly as a quick way to help them revise. The **Review quiz** activity is best done in pairs or groups or even with the whole class divided into two teams. You could even award points and score it as if it was a real TV quiz show!

Finally, the last section of each **Review, Learner advice,** looks at different strategies for learning the many expressions that students see in the Coursebook. While at lower levels students need to see how they can do more with a limited vocabulary, at the intermediate level students need to make a big leap in terms of the amount of vocabulary they have to learn in order to progress. Learning how to record and revise lexis is therefore a priority.

Each section has a short introduction to the technique, followed by an example and activity to practise it. All the language in these sections comes from the previous four units of the Coursebook and the corresponding units in the Workbook.

Tapescript

The Tapescript starts on page 148 and features all of the listening texts. Those texts which are also at the front of the Coursebook have the missing words and phrases highlighted in colour for easier identification. Where the grammar and vocabulary exercises use extended dialogues, they are in the tapescript. The reading texts and a number of other pronunciation and language exercises are also on the recording, but these do not appear in the tapescript in the Coursebook.

Photographs

Photographs play an important role throughout the Coursebook, and many exercises ask students very specifically to match vocabulary to photos (e.g. page 20), to role-play situations depicted in them (e.g. page 9), or to respond personally to them (e.g. page 97). Ideas about how to use photos like this are generally given in the explanation of a task, but additional ways to exploit the photos are given in individual unit notes in this book. The photos are also often there to help you explain some of the words students may ask about.

Language strips

Language strips as a resource

The language strips at the beginning of each unit provide valuable input which can be exploited in many different ways. They are particularly useful as a source of five-minute filler activities, between more substantial activities or at the end of a lesson. You should not, however, try to explain all the language in the strip. Instead, try to ensure students notice and learn two or three expressions from each strip.

Language in the language strips

All the expressions in the language strips are correct, natural, usually spoken language. Nearly all of them are expressions students could use to talk about themselves, their opinions and their reactions. In *Innovations intermediate* many of the expressions are explicitly focused on in the unit, so they are a good way of pre-teaching or revising vocabulary. There are also a limited number of common idiomatic expressions which are connected to the topic but may not directly come up in the unit. These are often fun for students to know and learn. The notes for each unit give definitions and examples of these more idiomatic expressions. You may need to give some guidance about how students can find out about these expressions. For some of the more idiomatic ones, for example, *Just take my word for it*, in **Unit 3 Holidays**, tell students to look at the phrases at the end of the dictionary entry for the key word, in this case, *word*. If students are studying in an English-speaking country, you could also encourage them to go out and ask people about the expressions.

Using the language strips

Students could look at the strips alone, but they are probably best used for pair or small-group activities in class. Ask students to look through the strip themselves and to choose some expressions that look interesting and to find out more about them. They can share their information in small groups in a later part of the class. They can then do another activity related to the strip. The notes for each unit give specific questions you can ask but the following are some general ideas which can be used for most of the language strips:

1. Ask students to find the expressions:
   a. which are responses to two or three questions or remarks you write on the board.
   b. which they could use about themselves.

2. Copy some of the expressions onto an overhead transparency, leaving some gaps. Ask students to complete the expressions before opening their Coursebooks, and then compare their answers with the expressions in the language strip.

3. Ask students to identify expressions:
   a. which contain a familiar idiom.
   b. which contain expressions with a phrasal verb.
   c. which contain language which has occurred in an earlier unit.

4. Ask students to sort the expressions in different ways:
   a. positive vs. negative expressions.
   b. formal vs. informal expressions.
   c. those which are more likely to be used by men/women.
   d. those which are more likely to be used by young/older people.
   e. remarks which initiate a conversation vs. responses.

Recording language

It is a good idea to help students organise a notebook to record the language they meet. Early on in the course, talk about recording this language in an organised way and suggest a notebook divided into several sections:

- a section organised alphabetically, containing not only the target words but associated collocations and phrases

- a section organised around themes such as describing people, work, films, etc.

- a section organised around 'delexicalised' verbs and nouns such as *get, take, point, thing*; a section for phrasal verbs

- a section for idioms; and a section for grammatical patterns and structures such as the present continuous and *was/were going to … but …* .

Also talk about what should be recorded. Instead of just isolated words, encourage the recording of complete phrases, collocations and even question/response exchanges. This Coursebook is a great resource of useful contextualised language that can be transferred directly to students' notebooks. Tell students to translate these larger expressions and idioms into an equivalent in their own language.

1 Getting to know you

Unit overview

General topic
Learning the language of introductions, asking questions, useful language-learning tips.

Reading
Students and teachers give tips on language learning.

Language input
- 'Getting to know you' questions: *Where are you from? What do you do when you're not working?* etc.
- Expressions for making personal questions more tentative; expressions we use when we do not wish to answer the question asked: *How old are you, if you don't mind me asking? I'd rather not say, if you don't mind.* etc.
- Some expressions for giving advice: *It's important to … , Don't worry too much about … .* etc.
- Collocations with common verbs: *give you some advice, make a mess, do a lot of damage,* etc.
- Past simple and past continuous in stories: *I was still packing when my taxi to the airport turned up!*

Language strip

Use the language strip as a way to lead in to the unit. Ask students to look quickly through the list and tell you in what situations these expressions might be used (e.g. getting to know someone at a party, in a class, over coffee, etc.). Ask if there are any expressions in the language strip that they've used in English before (*What do you do?* is one that they will probably suggest).

Then ask students to find two expressions that they haven't used before, but might use in the future. Explain that in this unit they will learn ways of asking and answering 'getting to know you' questions.

Use the language strip later on in this unit for a small group task. Ask students to choose expressions that are questions (e.g. *Are you single?*) and come up with a possible response (e.g. *Yes, why do you ask?*). Then ask them to choose expressions that are responses (e.g. *Really! Do you?*) and come up with statements that might prompt them (e.g. *I do a bit of painting in my spare time.*)

You might need to explain some of the following expressions:
- If you say someone has a funny accent, you find their accent strange or amusing. For example: *I'm not sure where she's from. She's got a funny accent.*

- In Britain, people often say *I'm from up north* to mean that they are from the northern part of England. The opposite is *I'm from down south.* This reflects the geographical and historical divisions of England in particular. (In the US, people also say *out west* and *back east.*)
- You might say *Are all (Norwegians) like you?* when you find the person you are talking to appealing, and so it's often used as a kind of chat-up line. (However, it could be used with a different intonation when you don't find the person appealing.)

Remind students to record any of the expressions that they like in their notebooks.

Lead in

If this is the first time you've met your students, you could lead in to the first task by getting them in small groups to brainstorm questions that they would like to ask you. Give them several minutes to talk about and prepare the questions, and then have them ask you their questions. This will allow them to find out more about you, and it will also give you a chance to assess their language needs in this area.

Using vocabulary

1 Fact-finding

The first task focuses on typical 'getting to know you' questions, many of which students will be familiar with. However, there are questions here that some students may have difficulty forming correctly (e.g. *Are you married?*) or expressing in a natural way (e.g. *What do you do when you're not working?*).

Have students work on the task individually before having them check with a partner. Once they have completed the task on their own, divide students into pairs and have one person say each of the questions 1–6 and the other give the appropriate response a–f. Then students swap roles for questions 7–12. This will enable you to monitor their pronunciation. When going through the answers, model the appropriate intonation and stress of the questions and have the class practise along with you.

Answers

1. do   2. Where   3. When   4. not   5. Do   6. Are
1. d.   2. a.   3. b.   4. f.   5. c.   6. e.

7. How   8. are   9. long   10. much   11. Have   12. been
7. h.   8. g.   9. j.   10. k.   11. l.   12. i.

You might want to draw your students' attention to how several of the answers are not specific. Have the class tell you which answers are not specific and write on the board the expressions that make them so:

we're thinking about it
nothing much
that kind of thing
on and off

2 | Speaking

Get students into small groups and have them go back through the questions, deciding which questions belong to which situation. Answers will vary, of course, but the following would generally be considered appropriate for each situation:

Answers

Possible answers:
The first time you meet: 1, 2, 9, 11, 12
Once you know each other a little better: 4, 5, 6, 7, 8
Once you know each other really well: 3, 10

After discussing their answers, have students talk about the last two questions in this exercise. In a multilingual class, you might want to extend this by getting them to talk about other questions that are culturally inappropriate.

Real English

Go over the note on answering questions with the class. Then ask students to go back to **1 Fact-finding** and notice how many responses were not full sentences. Point out that in response 'f', *I* is omitted. This is an example of ellipsis, which is quite common in spoken English.

Also draw students' attention to the way we can politely refuse to answer a question, and have students practise saying the expression *I'd rather not say if you don't mind*, in response to questions like *How much do you earn?* or *How old are you?*

3 | More personal questions

This exercise gives students a way of making a personal question more tentative. Let students read the examples and then play the recording once all the way through, stopping after each example so that they can practise saying it themselves. Ask them to think of two or three other questions that can be made more tentative using this language. Have students go around the class asking other members of the class the questions they've formulated. Remind them that they may politely refuse to answer questions with *I'd rather not say, if you don't mind*.

4 | Speaking

This will provide students with the chance to use the questions from **1 Fact-finding** to find out more about their classmates. Have them get into groups and start talking to each other. Ask questions 1–7 in **4 Speaking** to wrap up at the end of the exercise. Students may have already asked these questions when they were talking to each other during the first half of the exercise, so it may not be necessary to discuss them all.

For the second task, explain that students should move around the class talking to different people, getting to know them. After a few minutes, shout out 'Change!' and get them to talk to someone new. Take part in this activity yourself. You could even give this more of a party atmosphere by playing some music as students are mingling. To wrap up, write these expressions on the board and explain them:

We've got a lot in common.
I've got a lot in common with …
We don't have much in common.

Ask a few students to tell you about some of the people they talked to, using these phrases.

5 | Listening

Set the scene of the dialogue and ask students what questions they think would be asked. Ask if there are any questions that would not be asked by a man to a woman and vice versa. Then play the recording as students tick off the questions. Have them compare answers with a classmate before playing the recording again.

Answers

What do you do?
How long have you been here? (So, were you here last term?)
Where are you from? (You're not from here originally, though, are you?)

Working with the same partner, students now try to recall what they know about Jack and Lisa. You could turn this task into more of a role play, where they tell each other about a person (Jack or Lisa) that they've just met. Write an opening on the board to get them started:

Oh, by the way, did I tell you that I met this interesting person the other day? Jack, his name was.

6 Role play

For this role play have students choose one of the people in the photos. Give them five minutes to imagine what that person's life is like (e.g. their job, marital status, family, etc.).

Before students start, have them quickly look through the language strip on page 8 for more ideas of questions to ask. Have them spend about five minutes with another student before speaking to someone else. Go around the class yourself, monitoring and collecting examples of difficulties to go over when they've finished.

Reading

1 Speaking (The secret of success)

The purpose of this reading text is for students to reflect on ways that will help them in their language learning. It is also a chance for them to hear about the methodology behind this Coursebook.

Begin by having students complete the five sentence starters individually, and then have them share their ideas with a partner. Ask several students to tell the class some of their ideas. Point out that these sentence starters are useful for giving advice. Encourage students to record the patterns and a few examples, either their own or those they see in the reading text, into their notebooks.

Explain the reading task and tell students not to worry about understanding everything. When they have finished, get them in small groups to discuss their reactions. Give them a few sentence starters on the board:
I thought the advice about … was very useful …
I'm not sure I agree with …'s advice about …
I don't really understand the advice about …
I didn't understand what he/she meant by '…'

Allow students to spend some time talking in groups before discussing their ideas as a class. This is your chance to reinforce some of the advice in the reading text and to see their reaction to these kinds of ideas. If students ask about collocation, you can explain that the next task will deal with it in more detail.

2 Common verb collocations

This exercise helps students understand the concept of collocation and how it should play an important part in their language learning.

Have students work through the task first, and check their answers. You may need to explain that if you ask someone to *give you a hand* you are asking them to help

you, and that if someone *is going grey*, their hair is turning grey. Ask students to apply any of these collocations to the pictures on page 11. You could also encourage them to go back through the reading text, underlining any collocations they find.

Answers

1. give   2. make   3. do   4. get   5. go

Picture A: go grey
Picture B: do a lot of damage
Picture C: give me a hand with my homework
Picture D: do some research

Once students have completed the task, spend a short time talking about collocation and how it will affect their language learning. Ask students to think of examples of collocations in their own language to show that it is not something that just applies to English. Reinforce the point that it's useful to learn language in units bigger than single words by pointing out that it would be difficult to translate the verb *make* but much easier to translate *make a mess*.

Tell students that they should look out and listen for collocations all the time. Teach them classroom questions like the following:
What are some other collocations for … ?
Can you give me another collocation for … ?
Is this a good collocation for … ?

Tell students that whenever they record a new word in their notebooks, they should also include some collocations. This might also be a good opportunity to talk about special collocation dictionaries, and how to find common collocations in regular dictionaries. Demonstrate by asking if they can find some adjective collocations for the noun *issue*. (*A big issue* appears in the reading text; other words that collocate with *issue* are *important, complex, environmental*.)

3 Classroom language

The focus here is on the kinds of things you'll be asking students to do and the reasons for them. Students can work individually on the matching task. After checking the answers, allow time for the class to ask about and discuss these ideas.

Answers

1. e.   2. a.   3. b.   4. f.   5. c.   6. d.

You might want to point out the patterns to express reasons:
do this so that you (can) do that
do this to do that

Ask students to use these patterns to talk about some of the things they do in learning a language. For example: *I always write new vocabulary on note cards and carry them around, so that I can test myself when I'm on the bus.*

4 A quick quiz

This task focuses on some more important aspects of learning: pronunciation and grammar. It's probably best to do each part step by step, allowing students to quickly compare answers when appropriate. Again, at the end, spend some time talking about how each part relates to students' own language learning.

For the first part, you may want to talk about how stress is conveyed in English. For some language groups, a lot of practice is needed in lengthening stressed syllables and shortening unstressed syllables – using a rubber band to stretch out on the stressed syllables can help. For the last part, you could ask students to talk about the differences in pairs.

Answers

1. collo<u>ca</u>tion em<u>barr</u>assed mi<u>sta</u>ke <u>sur</u>name
2. accent, coast, design, whereabouts
3. chocolate: two syllables; syllable: three syllables; vegetable: three syllables; vocabulary: five syllables
5. a. *How long are you staying here?* refers to the future (from this time forward), while *How long have you been here?* connects the past to now (from when you first arrived here to now).
   b. *I've been studying English for six years* indicates an uninterrupted action or state and tells us that the person has been studying English continuously for six years, while *I've been studying English for six years on and off* indicates an interrupted action or state and tells us that the person took a break here and there.
   c. *What do you do?* is usually used to ask what someone does for a living, while *What are you doing?* is usually used to ask someone to explain their actions at the moment of speaking.

Using grammar

1 Past simple and past continuous

This section helps students see how these two tenses are used in the context of storytelling. The past continuous is typically used to show the background of a story, while the past simple is used for the main action. Let students read through the first sentence and underline examples of the two tenses. Check that they can see how the past continuous is formed (*was/were* + *-ing* form) and that they know *told* is the past simple form of *tell*. Then go over the explanation and the two examples together. Have students identify the two tenses here too.

To help students understand the use of the two tenses visually, draw a big empty square on the board. Tell them that this is going to be the opening scene of a movie. Ask them to suggest the time of year and day (e.g. spring, late afternoon), and the weather (e.g. sunny). Have them suggest some background actions (e.g. birds singing, clouds drifting) and draw these. Then have students suggest some everyday activities for a person (e.g. sitting on a park bench, reading a book). Draw a person doing this. Next, explain that you want something unusual or important to happen suddenly. Have students make some suggestions and choose one to draw on the board (e.g. a swarm of killer bees appeared). Now tell the story. For example:
It was a nice spring afternoon in a quiet town. The sun was shining, the birds were singing. A few clouds were slowly drifting across a deep blue sky. Our hero was sitting on a park bench, reading a book, when all of a sudden, a huge swarm of killer bees appeared.

2 Matching

This exercise helps students develop a grammar rule or guideline based on the examples in the task. Have students work individually on the matching task. While going through the answers, ask a few questions focusing on the language used in the sentences. For example:
What or who else can 'turn up'? (my ex-husband/wife, an old friend)
Apart from noodles and coffee, what else can you (or the cat) knock over? (a vase, my wine)
Can you think of some more household tasks that we use 'do' with? (e.g. do the laundry, do the hoovering, do the gardening)
What would you do if you'd missed your girl/boyfriend's birthday?
Has anyone ever found something interesting down the back of the sofa?

Then get pairs of students to practise the examples, with one person saying the first half of the sentence and the other person saying the second half of the sentence. You may want to talk about the unstressed pronunciation of *was* in the past continuous before students do this.

Answers

1. c. 2. d. 3. a. 4. b. 5. g. 6. h. 7. e. 8. f.

Students can then complete the three 'grammar rules'. Go over these as a class. You may want to draw a timeline on the board to visually represent the interruption concept in the third 'rule'. Encourage students to transfer a few examples from this page of the Coursebook into their notebooks. You could point out a few other examples of useful language here, too: *the other day, accidentally knock … all over … , knock … off.*

Answers

1. (past) continuous
2. (past) simple
3. (past) continuous, (past) simple

3 Practice

Here students can apply the 'rules' they formed in **2 Matching** to the following task. Have students work in pairs or individually before checking their answers. Do this by reading the completed version of each text to the class. Then have students practise telling the stories to each other. You may need to talk about the phrasal verb *end up* and how it is often used to express a result.

Answers

1. **Skiing**
   a. went b. broke c. was going d. realised
   e. Tried f. ended up g. broke h. ended up

2. **Going home on the bus**
   a. was going b. got c. sat d. started e. Tried
   f. got g. gave up h. changed i. started j. was

3. **A stupid thing to do**
   a. happened b. was living c. was watching
   d. was enjoying e. decided f. wanted g. Turned
   h. asked i. stared j. realised k. felt

Real English

Talk about this before students do **4 Free practice**. Draw students' attention to the pattern and have them make sentences based on the pictures at the bottom of page 13. You could have them come up with other endings as well. For example:
I was in the middle of changing the baby's nappy when my wife announced that she was pregnant again.

Encourage students to record a couple of examples in their notebooks.

4 Free practice

One way to lead in to this task is to tell the class a personal story yourself. Use one of the prompts and have the class listen and ask you questions. If possible, record your story so that you can get the class to listen again for any useful language you used. Write any expressions on the board. Give students time to plan how they are going to tell their stories. Draw their attention to how the stories start in **3 Practice**. Write a possible starter on the board:
One of the strangest/funniest/most frightening things that has ever happened to me happened while I was …

Once students are ready, get them to move around the class, telling their stories to each other. They should tell their story two or three times to different people. Explain that they will be improving their performance each time. Wrap up by discussing who had the best story, and dealing with any language difficulties.

Follow-up

You could use the photographs at the bottom of page 13 to develop a role play. Have students choose one of the people in the pictures and develop a story based on one of the prompts in the **4 Free practice**. Alternatively, you could have them write the story.

2 Free time

Unit overview

General topic
Free-time activities and strange hobbies.

Reading
A German woman collects china elephants.

Language input

- Expressions for talking about evening activities: *I just stayed in and watched TV. I went out for dinner.* etc.

- Collocations with *club*: *a bridge club, join a club, a member of the local tennis club,* etc.

- Vocabulary for talking about interests: *I like anything by ... . I'm a big baseball fan. I try to go to the gym whenever I can.* etc.

- Present perfect continuous and past simple: *I've been playing tennis now for about five years. How long did you do that for?*

- Time expressions: *for quite a while now, for ages now,* etc.

- Present perfect continuous to talk about recent activities: *I've been looking after the kids the last few months.*

Language strip

Use the language strip as a way to lead in to the unit. Ask students to look quickly through the list and find any expressions that they could use themselves. Explain that in this unit they will learn ways of asking and talking about free-time activities. Encourage them to choose some expressions in the strip that look interesting and to find out more about them.

Use the language strip later on in this unit for a small group task. Ask students to imagine that they are at a party and are talking to someone they find really interesting. On their own, they should then choose the expressions they think might be used in such a conversation. They can then share their ideas with other group members.

You might need to explain some of the following expressions:

- You might say *I suppose I'm a bit boring, really* to say that you don't think you do anything exciting. For example: *I don't have any spare time. I work, work, work. I'm a bit boring, really.*

- You ask *What've you been up to?* to find out what someone has been doing recently. For example: *I haven't seen you for ages. What've you been up to?*

- If you *work out*, you do some physical exercise, usually in a gym.

Remind students to record any of the expressions that they like in their notebooks.

Lead in

Lead in to the first task by asking the class a few questions:
What do you do in your free time?
Do you have any free time?
What would you do if you had more free time?
If you had a couple of hours to spare, what would you do with them?

Using vocabulary

1 Evening activities

Use the pictures to find out whether anyone does or would like to do any of the activities shown. Tell the class a little about yourself, too.

This exercise gives students ways of talking about what they did in the evening. Introduce the first task by asking them to guess what you did last night. Then ask them about their evenings. Then go over the three patterns before having them complete the sentences 1–15.

Before you check their answers, model some of the patterns so that students can hear where you pause and which words you stress. Have them follow your pronunciation when giving their answers. Then allow them a couple of minutes to decide which of the activities are 'nothing much'. Point out the expressions *have an early night* and *take it easy*. Ask students what, for them, constitutes an early night and taking it easy. You might also want to ask them to find any verb + noun collocations they find interesting and record these in their notebooks.

Answers
1. b.   2. a.   3. b.   4. c.   5. a.   6. b.   7. c.   8. a.
9. b.   10. c.   11. a.   12. c.   13. a.   14. a.   15. c.
'Nothing much' activities: 1, 2, 5, 8, 11, 13, 14

For the next task, model the example conversation with one student. Then take the other part and repeat the conversation with another student. Students can then practise their own conversations in pairs. Have them do a few examples before getting two pairs together to perform their conversations for each other.

2 | Free practice

For this activity, get students to stand up and wander around, asking each other about what they did last night. Write some examples of questions that they can ask on the board before they start. For example:
Did you do anything interesting last night?
Did you do anything special last night?
Did you do anything much last night?

Wrap up by getting students to tell you about the most popular, most interesting and most unusual activity.

3 | Follow-up questions

It's important to point out that dialogues don't usually comprise just a question and response. It is a good idea to generally encourage students to use follow-up questions to keep conversations going. Also, when you ask your class questions or give them example conversations, try to add follow-up questions, too. Here students see some ways to follow up the conversations they had in **2 Free practice.**

Play the recording as students fill in the gaps. Replay the recording and stop after each question so students can practise saying them with the same stress and intonation pattern. Then have them work in pairs, matching the responses to the questions. Point out that there are two responses for each question. After students have checked their answers, say all the responses for the class and have students practise them, especially the way *all right* in 'd.' and *quite a bit* in 'e.' are said to give the appropriate meaning. Finish off by getting pairs of students to practise asking and answering the questions.

> **Answers**
>
> 1. often   2. long   3. that   4. very   5. any   6. any
>
> 1. e.   2. a.   3. f.   4. b.   5. c.   6. d.

You could also ask students to discuss what the conversations are about. For example, 4. b. might be a conversation about a club.

4 | Free practice

Here students have the opportunity to practise some of the language from the previous exercises. After they have made their list, give them a minute to look through the examples of follow-up questions. Remind students to invent some fun activities if they just stayed in last night. Again, get students to have conversations with several people. You might want to join in yourself. Before moving on to the next task, give students a few minutes to add any expressions that they like to their notebooks.

Reading

1 | An unusual hobby (An interview with Fritzi)

Lead in to the reading text by talking about hobbies in general, and then asking if anyone had an unusual hobby when they were a child, and whether they still keep it up. Remember to talk a little bit about yourself, too. Go through the introduction to the reading text and set the interview task. Have a few students tell you what they've come up with before letting the class read the text. Before moving on to the next task, play the recording of the interview so students can hear how the language sounds as they read along.

2 | Speaking

Have the original pairs of students confirm how many of their questions were answered before getting them to talk to another partner about how Fritzi answered their questions. Remind them to use their own words rather than keep referring to the text.

3 | Speaking

Here students talk about different kinds of clubs and what they might be interested in joining. Before having students work on this task, you may need to explain some of the clubs in the box. *A bridge club* is a club where people go to play the card game bridge. In *a debating club*, people argue in a formal way for one of two sides of an issue.

One way to do these tasks is to have students work on the first two individually before getting them to share their answers with a partner. Then give them a few minutes to think about the third task. Write some example sentence starters on the board to help them express their reasons:
It's a great place to …
You'll really enjoy the …
It's a fun way to …
It'll be good for your …

Students can then walk around the class, talking about their club. You could suggest that they start by talking about what they did last night. For example:
A: What did you do last night?
B: Oh, I went to my web design club.
A: Oh, yeah. How often do you do that, then?
B: Every week. It's a great club. You should join …

4 | Vocabulary focus

In this task, students are introduced to several useful expressions to talk about what they do in their free time. Have them work individually or in pairs, using dictionaries where necessary, before going through the answers.

Answers

1. a. get given   b. fairs   c. album   d. spare   e. swap
2. a. novels   b. anything by   c. anything on   d. browsing
3. a. pool   b. fifty lengths   c. front crawl   d. sauna
4. a. anything by   b. track   c. album   d. gigs   e. band
5. a. fan   b. support   c. games   d. stadium
6. a. fit   b. gym   c. running machine   d. weights   e. class

Then have students go back and find sentences to say about themselves or that they can adapt. Ask several students to tell you what they have come up with and write their sentences on the board. You may want to draw students' attention to the expressions *read/like anything by/on/about* and *that kind of thing*.

Using grammar

1 Present perfect continuous and past simple

The focus in this section is on how the present perfect continuous is used to talk about ongoing actions that started in the past, while the past simple is used to talk about completed past actions. The use of the present perfect continuous to talk about recent activities is also covered. While working through this section, remind students to record whole expressions as examples of the two tenses in their notebooks.

Lead in to the first task by talking about something you used to do and something you do now. For example: *I used to be really into rock climbing. I did it for about three years before I fell and broke my leg. I gave it up and started sailing instead. I've been doing it pretty regularly since then.*

Then have students look at the two examples and check that they understand that a is past simple and b is present perfect continuous before looking at the two example conversations. You may want to talk a little about how the present perfect continuous is formed and draw a timeline on the board to visually represent the examples.

Answers

Conversation 1 is like b (present perfect continuous).
Conversation 2 is like a (past simple).

2 Practice

In this exercise, students can apply what they noticed in **1 Present perfect continuous and past simple** to the dialogues. Students can work by themselves first before comparing their answers with a partner. Ask questions focusing on some of the other language as you check their answers. For example:

Does anyone here know how to do web design? Does anyone do karate? What other activities can we use 'do' with? (tai chi, origami)

What other expressions with 'I'm off' are commonly used to say we are leaving to go somewhere? (I'm off to work, I'm off home)

Is anyone here quite a good runner? How about a good basketball or football player?

Answers

1. How long have you been doing that, then?
2. How long have you been doing that, then?
3. How long did you do that for, then?
4. How long did you do that for, then?
5. How long have you been doing that, then?
6. How long did you do that for, then?

3 Pronunciation: sounding interested

A lot of the meaning is conveyed by the way we say something. Say the first example with different intonation patterns and pitch levels and ask students to tell you what emotion they convey (boredom, impatience, surprise and suspicion are possible examples). Then play the recording and have students practise the intonation and pitch level for sounding interested before getting them to practise the conversations in **2 Practice** in pairs.

4 Time expressions

Students may have learnt a rule that *for* and *since* are used with the present perfect continuous. Although these two words are frequently used with the present perfect, they are used with other tenses too: *for* is used to describe a length of time and is common with other tenses (e.g. *I worked for about three years, I'll be here three more months*); *since* means starting from a point in the past and continuing until now or another point in the past and is usually used in perfect tenses (e.g. *I was feeling exhausted because I'd been working non-stop since the start of the month*).

Another rule that students may have learnt is that *for* is used with periods of time and *since* with points of time. This is certainly one way of learning the difference, but encourage students to also learn these words in larger phrases. Suggest that they have a page in their notebook where they collect *for* and *since* expressions. After having students complete the task and checking their answers, tell them to go back and underline the complete time expressions.

Answers

The wrong time expressions are:

1. when I was at high school

2. two years ago

3. when I was in Canada

4. when I was a kid

5. last month

6. before my computer died

7. ages ago

8. two years ago

The two words associated with the present perfect are *for* and *since*.

5 Free practice

This exercise gives students the chance to personalise the language from the previous exercises. Before they start completing the sentences, ask for a few examples of things that we *play*, *do* and *go (to)* and write them on the board:

play + football, bridge, the piano
do + karate, web design, folk dancing
go + to dance classes, to see films, running

For the second task, give an example of the kinds of questions students could ask. Do the first one as an example with a student:

A: *I've been learning English on and off for thirteen years.*

B: *Thirteen years. That's a long time. How old were you when you started?*

A: *Eleven, I think.*

B: *Is it common to start learning at that age?*

A: *It used to be. Now a lot of children start learning English at six or seven.*

6 Talking about recent activities

The present perfect continuous is also used to talk about recent actions that have been happening over an extended period of time. It is therefore common to use it in answers to the question *What have you been up to?* Go through the example and have students practise saying it with you, reminding them to use the contracted form *I've*. As you go through the answers, point out the useful verb + noun collocations: *work overtime, revise for my exams, do my flat up, look after the kids, try to find a new job*. Ask students what *doing up a flat* might involve (e.g. *fixing things, painting the walls*).

Answers

1. I've been working a lot of overtime recently.

2. I've been revising for my exams for the last few weeks.

3. I've been doing my flat up for the last month.

4. I've been sorting out my summer holiday for the last few days.

5. I've been looking after the kids for the last few months.

6. I've been trying to find a new job recently.

Refer students to the **Real English** note on *I've been busy -ing*. Ask them to reformulate the answers in **6 Talking about recent activities** using this structure. You could also teach them the expression *long time, no see*, which would also be appropriate in this context. Then have pairs of students practise the conversations, encouraging them to keep each conversation going with follow-up questions.

Follow-up

As a follow-up to this unit, ask students to think of a strange hobby and to write it on a slip of paper. Collect all the slips, mix them up and hand out a slip to each student. Tell them that they have this strange hobby and that they are going to be interviewed about it. Get the students in pairs to role-play interviews with each other, like the one with Fritzi on page 16. In addition to the questions used in the text, write some other ideas on the board:

What made you start collecting … ?
What's so interesting about … ?
Have you been doing it long?
Don't people find it odd?
What do your friends say about it?

Once students have practised this in pairs, get them to perform their interviews in bigger groups.

3 Holidays

Unit overview

General topic
Holidays and places to visit.

Dialogue
Rose and Steve talk about their holiday plans.

Language input
- Vocabulary to describe holidays and holiday activities: *We had a week in Paris. We went walking quite a lot. It was really good value for money.* etc.
- Things you can rent and hire: *rent a car, rent a flat, hire a bike,* etc.
- Expressions with *place: It's a great place to go skiing. I couldn't find a place to park.* etc.
- Present perfect and past simple: *Have you ever been to Ibiza? No, but I've always wanted to. The scenery was fantastic.* etc.
- Position of adverbs: *We've just heard the news. We've always been good friends. I really don't like it.*
- Contrastive stress: *No, never, but I <u>have</u> been to Hong Kong. Yes, I <u>have</u>, actually.*

Language strip

Use the language strip as a way to lead in to the unit. Ask students to look quickly through the list and find any expressions that they might have used about a holiday they have been on. Explain that in this unit they will learn ways of asking and talking about holidays. Encourage them to choose some other expressions in the strip that look interesting and to find out more about them.

Use the language strip later on in this unit for a small group task. Ask students to sort the expressions into those that refer to the past (e.g. *It rained the whole time*) and those that refer to the present or future (e.g. *Where are you going this year?*).

You might need to explain some of the following expressions:

- *Ever been camping?* is another example of ellipsis; *have you* has been dropped. This form is common in spoken English.
- You say *just take my word for it* to tell someone to accept what you're saying without your having to go into a lot of detail to explain why what you are saying is true. For example: *You'll regret not taking out health insurance, just take my word for it.*

- You say *It's time we had a break* when you want to go away somewhere to relax. For example: *We've been working a lot recently. I think it's time we had a break. Let's go away for the weekend.* In the example above, notice that after we say *It's time*, we use a past tense to talk about the present/future.
- If a holiday is *self-catering*, you do the cooking yourself.
- *You're a little red on the shoulders* means your shoulders are slightly sunburnt – maybe you didn't use enough sun cream!

Remind students to record any of the expressions that they like in their notebooks.

Lead in

To lead in to this unit, tell students about one of the best holidays you have ever had or one of the worst. Encourage them to ask you questions. Then ask them to recall any interesting expressions you used and write them on the board. Follow up by asking if a few students would like to tell the class about a holiday experience.

Using vocabulary

1 Speaking

In this section, students focus on expressions for different holiday activities. Start off by asking them to match the sentences 1–8 to the photographs A–H on page 20 as a way of checking their understanding. You may need to explain that *a fortnight* is short for *fourteen nights,* so two weeks. Point out the patterns here: *we went on … , we went -ing,* and *we had (a fortnight in the sun).*

Have students discuss the questions in pairs. Go over the stuctures used for guessing and model their pronunciation. Explain that *I reckon* is an informal way of saying *I think.* Then ask which of the structures shows less certainty. *(It looks like it could be … or somewhere like that.)*

Answers			
1. d	3. c	5. h	7. a
2. e	4. g	6. f	8. b

2 Holiday activities

To lead into this task, divide the class into groups. Assign each group one of the holidays shown in the pictures. Ask them to brainstorm the kind of activities someone might do on such a holiday.

Have students individually mark the activities. You may need to explain that *the locals* means *the local people*. (You could also tell them that *the local* means *the local pub* in British English.) Point out that *go clubbing* refers to dance clubs. Before students compare answers, talk about and practise the short dialogue. Make sure students hear how *I* is stressed in *So/neither do I* and *I'm afraid I don't*. You could also point out that *Me too* can be used instead of *So do I*.

As an extension, have students form new pairs and imagine that they have just been on holiday with their previous partner. Tell them to role-play a conversation with a friend about their time together. Write a few expressions on the board to help:
We had a great time.
We got on really well together.
We liked doing the same things.
We both did our own thing.
We could never agree on what to do.
We ended up doing nothing.
It was a nightmare.

3 Vocabulary practice

The six texts here are full of useful expressions for talking about holidays. After students have finished filling in the gaps, get them to underline any expressions that they feel they could use in the future. Demonstrate what is meant by 'the complete expression' with an example from the first text: *we went out on shopping trips (to the market)*. Remind them to record these expressions in their notebooks.

One way to help reinforce the language is in a pair work activity. One person reads the text aloud, stopping at the blanks while the other person tries to remember the missing word without looking at the Coursebook. Have pairs of students take turns reading and remembering.

Answers
1. a. stayed b. trips c. out d. went
2. a. camping b. campsite c. went d. tent
3. a. went b. round c. took d. rucksack
4. a. self-catering b. cottage c. fire d. cooking
5. a. package b. value c. flight d. sitting
6. a. cruise b. scenery c. bored d. again

As a model for the second task, tell the class about the last holiday you went on. Then give students time to prepare to talk about their holiday. Have them practise telling two other students.

Listening

1 Speaking

The questionnaire in the Coursebook is meant to prepare students for the listening task. You could have the class ask you the questions first, before they ask each other The reporting-back task gives you a chance to assess your students' abilities in forming the present perfect.

2 While you listen (Summer holidays)

Read the instructions for this task aloud (page 22) to help students prepare for the listening activity. Ask them to listen for the answers to the two questions that follow. Then play the recording, making sure that they cover the text. Ask them to discuss answers in pairs, making sure that students keep the text covered as they do this. Next, let them read the conversation as you play the recording again. Students may work in pairs to fill in as many gaps as they can from memory. Play the recording through one more time, with students following the text, this time with pauses, so that they can check and fill in the missing words.

If you want students to read the conversation, or parts of it, in pairs, use the tapescript on page 148. The missing words are in colour.

Answers
1. Steve is going camping in Portugal. Rose hasn't decided yet. She may go to Ibiza or Cornwall.
2. Steve hasn't been before. Rose went to Cornwall last year. She hasn't been to Ibiza, but a friend has.

Words in gaps in the conversation:
1. Whereabouts
2. rent a car
3. supposed to be
4. give it a try
5. cheap offers
6. a cottage
7. to be honest
8. get some sun
9. package holidays
10. worth a try

Depending on your class, you may need to explain a little about the places mentioned. Ibiza is an island off the coast of Spain and is a very popular tourist destination, particularly for young British people. It's one of the party capitals of Europe and is famous for its nightlife. Cornwall is in the southwest of England. It is very rural and has a lot of beaches and spectacular coastal scenery. It often gets the warmest weather in summer.

3 Vocabulary

This exercise focuses on some of the expressions that appeared in the conversation **Summer holidays.** As you go through the answers, try to ask a few more questions to help extend the students' vocabularies. For example:

Do you prefer going abroad on holiday or staying in your own country?

Can you think of some other ways to complete the expression 'I'm not exactly sure …'? (why you're here, how to answer this question, what this means)

Apart from a flight, what else can you 'book'? (a ticket, a seat, a room)

Can you make some other sentences using the structure 'What do you think the … is/are going to be like?' to talk about things on a holiday? (the locals, the food, the hotel)

Have students record the expressions that they like in their notebooks. You may need to explain the following expression. If you *give a place a try* or say *a place might be worth a try,* you are thinking about visiting a place you've never been to before. For example: *Why don't we give that new Thai restaurant a try? I've heard it's supposed to be good.*

Answers

1. going   2. sure   3. going   4. booked   5. rent
6. supposed   7. give   8. like   9. package   10. worth

Finish up by asking pairs of students to discuss the last three questions in the exercise. If they haven't been to any of the places mentioned in the conversation, brainstorm a list of other popular tourist destinations. If they have heard about a place from a friend, they can use *It's supposed to be … .* Write some expressions to describe places on the board:

It's (supposed to be) a great place to/for …
It's (supposed to be) quite …
It's (supposed to be) very …
It's a bit too … for my liking.
There are too many …
There aren't enough …

You might also want to tell students about the negative adjective *touristy* to describe a place with a lot of tourists. Ask them to tell you some examples of places that have become too touristy.

4 Speaking

Refer students to the **Real English** note on *rent* and *hire* before completing the speaking task. Share a personal story about a time you rented any of these things. (This is a good opportunity to review the use of the past continuous and past simple.) Here is an example story if you don't have one yourself:

I was on holiday in Bali a few years ago and my friend and I decided to hire a couple of bikes and ride around a bit. We rode quite a distance from our hotel and it was getting late, so we decided to head home. While we were riding fast down this steep hill, I suddenly saw a cat in the road and swerved to avoid it. I ended up in a ditch with the front wheel of the bike broken. We were miles from anywhere and hadn't seen anyone on the road for hours. We didn't know what to do. Then I noticed a small house near the road. I knocked on the door to ask for help. It turned out that the person living there was a bicycle repair man! He fixed my bike and I was back on the road in no time!

Explain that we use *a villa* to describe a large-ish house, especially in southern Europe, while *a cottage* is smaller and found in the country. (You could also mention *wood cabins* in the mountains or *chalets* in ski resorts.)

To follow up you could have students think about how they would go about renting one of these things in English. Form them into pairs to write a dialogue and then role-play the conversation.

5 Odd one out

This is a fun activity that not only tests students' knowledge of geography, but introduces vocabulary for different places. You can also talk a little about which names use *the*. If students come up with different answers, ask them to explain why. They may be right!

Answers

a. Mexico: It isn't a US state. (An alternative answer is New York: It was never owned by the Spanish.)

b. Shanghai: It isn't a capital city. (An alternative answer is Buenos Aries: It isn't in the northern hemisphere,)

c. Edinburgh: It isn't in England. It's in Scotland.

d. The Nile: It isn't a lake. It's a river.

e. Kilimanjaro: It isn't a mountain range. It's a mountain.

In the next task, students work on how these places are pronounced in English. Play the recording twice, while students mark the stress. Then check their answers by having students say the names. Follow up with the questions, either as a whole class or in small groups.

Answers

The Hima<u>la</u>yas   The Py<u>re</u>nees   <u>Mi</u>chigan   <u>E</u>dinburgh
Vic<u>to</u>ria   Kiliman<u>ja</u>ro   Ge<u>ne</u>va   Copen<u>ha</u>gen
Slo<u>ve</u>nia   <u>Bue</u>nos <u>Ai</u>res   <u>Chi</u>le   <u>Bru</u>ssels

6 Expressions with *place*

The noun *place* occurs in many different expressions. Encourage students to devote a single page in their notebooks for those expressions they find here and any others they may encounter. Have students work in pairs before you check their answers. Ask them further questions as you do so. For example:

Do you know of a good French place near here?

Would you ever invite me over to your place?

Where's a great place to go surfing/camping/scuba diving?

How long would you save someone's place in a crowded coffee shop?

Where's the best place to park around here?

Do you leave things all over the place?

> **Answers**
>
> Possible answers:
> 1. a restaurant   2. Nick's home   3. any ski resort; Swiss Alps, Austria, Colorado, etc.   4. a seat/place in a queue   5. a locked drawer/a safety deposit box   6. a cottage   7. a parking space   8. a flat/house   9. the floor   10. a garden/yard

After students have finished discussing the second task, have a few students tell their ideas to the whole class. Point out the two patterns:

a (adjective) place to (verb)

a (adjective) place for a (noun)

Encourage them to record a couple of their examples for each one in their notebooks.

Using grammar

1 Present perfect: the best rule

Students will remember from the previous unit that the present perfect continuous is used to talk about ongoing actions that started in the past and also, to talk about recent activities. Here the basic concept of the present perfect as a present tense looking back into the past is reinforced.

Have students look through the examples individually and then choose the best explanation. They can then compare their answers with a partner before thinking of other examples of the present perfect. This task therefore helps students draw their own conclusion to explain the basic function of the present perfect. Finish by discussing their conclusions and examples as a whole class. You may want to represent the basic idea of the present perfect visually on the board, along with a few of the class's examples.

> **Answers**
>
> Explanation b is true for all three examples. Both a and c could explain the first and third sentences, respectively.

2 Asking questions

Some traditional grammar books have students practise answering questions in the present perfect with just *Yes, I have* or *No, I've never been to … .* The examples here are more realistic. After students look through the examples, have them work individually adding *no* or *yes*. Then play the recording, stopping after each one to allow students to repeat the answer, following the same stress and intonation patterns.

> **Answers**
>
> 1. No   2. No   3. Yes   4. Yes   5. Yes   6. No   7. Yes   8. No   9. Yes   10. No

Before moving on to the next task, have students sort the answers into positive (1, 2, 4, 6), neutral (5, 10) and negative (3, 7, 8, 9). Demonstrate the speaking task, with a student asking you questions first. Reply using some of the structures in 1–10.

Then have students work in pairs, asking each other if they've visited the places on the list. Encourage them to talk a little about places they've been to. Alternatively, or during a review later, write the names of the countries on slips of paper and hand out one to each student. Have each student find someone to ask about the place on their slip. When students have finished talking, they can exchange their slips and find another person to ask about the place on their new slip.

3 Free practice

The present perfect is often used to ask about general experience. If we have an experience and want to give details, we typically switch to the past simple, as our focus has shifted away from the general period of time up to now to a specific time in the past.

Go through the example with the class, perhaps asking if anyone has been on a cruise. If someone has, ask them to give you details about it.

You may need to explain that if someone *goes backpacking* they are travelling independently, usually staying in cheap places and carrying everything in a backpack, while if someone goes on *a package holiday*, everything like the flight and accommodation is arranged by a company beforehand. You could develop this into a discussion on cruises, backpacking, package holidays and camping in general. You may ask questions such as these to prompt class participation:

What are some good things/bad things about these holidays?

What things could go wrong?

What sort of people take these holidays?

You could also divide the class up into four groups with each group assigned one of these holidays. They should come up with reasons why theirs would make the ideal holiday. Finally, form small groups of four made up of one person from each of the original groups and have them try to convince each other that their holiday is best.

Answers

The past simple was used in the answer.

---

4 Position of adverbs

The adverbs in this list are commonly, though, of course, not exclusively, used with the present perfect. Have students work through sentences 1–6 and then check their answers. Then find out how many people can say they've never been to Canada or eaten squid and always liked the British or have always wanted to go to India. Ask students what the opposite of these four sentences would be. *(I've been to Canada. I've eaten squid. I've never liked the British. I've never wanted to go to India.)*

Answers

1. I've never been to the south of Italy.
2. We've just heard the news.
3. We've always been good friends.
4. I've already seen that film twice.
5. Have you seen their new baby yet?
6. Has she ever been married?

For the next activity, students should spend a few minutes preparing their lists. Before they talk to their partner, tell them about some of the things in your personal list so they can listen to the way you talk about it.

Real English

Draw students' attention to how the position of *really* changes meanings of sentences. First, model the two examples for the class. Then ask questions such as the ones below and have students practise the expressions when they respond. For example:

What do you think of the weather here?

What do you think of my shirt?

What do you think of the way Liverpool play football?

Answers

I really don't like it is stronger.

---

5 Pronunciation: contrastive stress

This exercise gives students another example of how stress is used in English pronunciation. Play the recording so students can hear how *have* is stressed, before having them practise as a class and in pairs. Then have pairs of students talk about the places in the list. Remind students to provide more details in their responses (as in the recording), and to use follow-up questions to keep the conversation going. You may want to do the first one as an example:

A: *Have you ever been to Barcelona?*

B: *No, never, but I have been to Madrid.*

A: *Oh, really? What was it like?*

B: *Brilliant! The weather was great, the people were really nice.*

Follow-up

Ask students prepare a talk on one of the following topics:

The longest trip I've ever taken

The best holiday I've ever had

The worst holiday I've ever had

The most fun I've ever had on holiday

The best holiday I had when I was a kid

Have them spend some time preparing what they want to say, and then get them to tell their story a few times to different people. Alternatively, bring in some travel brochures or advertisements for package holidays and adventure trips and have pairs of students imagine they have gone on this holiday together, talking about what they did. They then go around talking to other people, trying to convince them to join them on the same holiday next year.

4 Feelings

Language strip

Use the language strip as a way to lead in to the unit. Ask students to quickly look through the list and find any expressions that they have or could have actually used themselves. Then explain that in this unit they will learn ways of talking about feelings. Encourage them to choose some other expressions in the strip that look interesting and to find out more about them.

Use the language strip later on in this unit for a small group task. Ask students to sort the expressions into two categories: those that might be used in a bad situation (e.g. *I'm really sorry to hear that*) and those that might be used in a good situation (e.g. *What a surprise!*). Alternatively, ask students to choose several of the expressions that are questions (e.g. *What's the matter?*) and come up with a possible response (e.g. *I'd rather not talk about it, if you don't mind*). Then ask them to choose several of the expressions that are responses (e.g. *I'm really sorry to hear that*) and come up with statements that might prompt them (e.g. *I've just had some bad news, My father's been taken into hospital.*)

You might need to explain some of the following expressions:

- If you are *fed up*, you are unhappy because something bad has been going on for a long time – or has happened again and again and again.
  For example: *I'm really fed up with this rain.*

- If someone is *not your cup of tea*, they aren't the kind of person you find appealing. For example: *He's quite nice, but he's not really my cup of tea. I'm looking for someone a bit more outgoing.*

- If you are *irritated*, you are angry or annoyed. For example: *I'm really irritated with him at the moment. I lent him my screwdriver and he's gone and lost it.*

Remind students to record any of the expressions that they like in their notebooks.

Lead in

To lead in to this unit, ask the class to think of different greetings that they've heard in English. For example:
How's it going?
How are you?
What's up?
All right?
How have you been doing?
How have you been?
What's happening?

List them on the board and ask students for different ways to answer them. Ask if they use or would use any of the greetings themselves.

Reading

1 How's it going? (The day that changed my life)

In this exercise, students focus on ways to answer the common greeting *How's it going?* Often we answer this question with *OK, Not bad,* or *Good*. However, if we feel different from this standard response and we want to talk about it, we sometimes use *actually* or *to be honest* in our answer and then explain why we feel that way.

Have students do the matching task and check their answers before working with a partner on other possible endings. Get them to tell you a few of their suggestions. Point out the use of *actually* and *to be honest* and then have pairs of students practise asking *How's it going?* and answering with 1–4. Model the conversations and have the class follow your stress and intonation. You may want to practise the way *How's it going?* is said like one word. They can then work on their own conversations following the model in the Coursebook. Remind them that they can keep the conversation going if they wish. Explain that *How come ... ?* is another way of asking *Why ... ?*

Answers

1. b.   2. c.   3. d.   4. a.

You could talk about the use of *sick* and *ill*. In the follow-up comment 'd.', *sick of* means that you are extremely unhappy with something that's been going on for a long time, whereas in number 1, *ill* means *not feeling well*.

Ask students to look at the title of the reading text and to suggest examples of events that could change someone's life. Ask if anyone would like to tell the class about a day that changed their life. Then explain that they will read an article about how a couple met. They should read the article and then share their reactions with a partner. Tell them not to worry about understanding everything. Write a few sentence starters on the board to help:
I think this is a … story because …
I felt really … when I read this because …
I think they'll stay together because …
I don't think the relationship will last because …

After students have discussed their reactions, play the recording and let them listen and read at the same time. They can underline any expressions they find interesting, either while or after they listen. You might want to point out that there are several expressions dealing with emotions and feelings. Have students compare the expressions they chose with a partner. Encourage them to record these in their notebooks.

2 | True or false?

This exercise focuses on some of the expressions in the text. Have students work individually first and then compare and explain their answers in pairs. Encourage them to use expressions in the text to support their opinions.

Answers

1. False. They met when they were at school together.
2. False. She just did it on impulse.
3. False. Jim has fought hard to overcome his addictions.
4. False. Andrea's parents wanted her to marry someone with money.
5. False. Jim doesn't see it this way, but even now it still makes Andrea angry the way the papers and the TV producers treat people.

3 | Speaking

Use these questions to follow on from the reading task. You may need to explain that *exploiting* someone means using them for some purpose and not giving them much in return. Ask students to give you some more examples of exploitation. You might also need to explain that if someone *finds religion* they become religious.

4 | Expressions with *get*

Refer students to the **Real English** note on *get* and *become* before doing the matching task. In this exercise, students focus on several expressions with *get*, many of which are negative (e.g. *get killed*, *get evicted*). If students haven't done so already, encourage them to record the expressions with *get* on a separate page in their notebooks. Explain that if you *get evicted*, you are forced to move out from the home you are renting, and that if you *get sacked*, you are fired from your job. Ask students to give some reasons why a manager might sack someone.

Answers

1. f.   2. d.   3. c.   4. b.   5. a.   6. e.   7. h.   8. g.

5 | Speaking

Introduce the task by telling students about the last wedding you went to. Have them discuss the questions with a partner, and then ask if they would like to share their thoughts with the rest of the class.

6 | Free practice

Have students spend some time preparing their story before sharing it with their partner. Encourage them to add extra details that were not included in the reading text. You may want to suggest that the person listening take an active part in the conversation by responding with comments like *I see. Really? Oh, how awful* as well as questions like *Why was that? When was that? How come?* They should then retell their stories to another pair of students.

Using vocabulary

1 | Adjectives with two different forms

Students often have problems with the *-ing* and *-ed* forms of adjectives. Although they are helped in establishing a set of 'guidelines', remind them that they should learn examples of the two forms in larger phrases and patterns.

Draw students' attention to the two examples from the text and ask if anyone can remember why Andrea said them (she was surprised because she burst out crying; the hostel was depressing). Have students discuss the questions about rules with a partner before they complete the pairs of sentences 1–8. You might want to point out that we can use the *-ing* form *interesting* to describe people, too (e.g. *I thought he was a really interesting guy*).

As you go through the answers, tell students to underline whole expressions. For example: *I'm still a bit confused about it. He's got this really annoying habit. I'm absolutely terrified of heights.*

Answers

1.	a. confused	b. confusing
2.	a. annoying	b. annoyed
3.	a. depressing	b. depressed
4.	a. Terrifying	b. Terrified
5.	a. worrying	b. worried
6.	a. surprised	b. surprising
7.	a. frustrated	b. frustrating
8.	a. boring	b. bored

Students can then write their own examples for the five other adjective pairs. As they are working on this, go around the class checking and helping. Ask several students to share some of their sentences. Here are some possible answers if students ask for them:

I was terribly disappointed to learn that I hadn't got the job.

I found 'The Matrix Reloaded' a bit disappointing.

I'm tremendously excited about working in the city.

It really is an exciting time to be living in London.

I was scared to death he would find out that I'd lost the bracelet he'd given me.

Hang-gliding can be a bit scary at first, but you'll get used to it.

He gets all stressed-out when there is a deadline to meet.

This job can be really stressful, but the pay is good.

I was pretty upset by the television images of the war.

I found those images too upsetting, so I don't watch the news.

You could also talk about some of the adverb collocations for these adjectives, like *tremendously excited* in the example above.

2 Speaking

These questions will help reinforce the language learned in **1 Adjectives with two different forms**. First, divide students into pairs or small groups. Before they begin the exercise, tell them some things that worry or terrify you. You could also talk about habits that you find annoying. Teach students the phrase *I hate/don't like it when people (spit on the street/put gum on chairs/put their feet up on seats).* Ask small groups or pairs to report back some of their ideas.

3 Collocations

Here the focus is explicitly on adjective + noun collocations, some of which have appeared in the previous exercises. Remind students that they should choose the list in which all of the nouns correctly collocate with the adjectives. Once you have checked their answers, have them discuss good examples of those collocations that are new to them. As always, encourage students to record these collocations in their notebooks.

You may need to explain that *the plot* of a novel or a film is the story. We can talk about *a complex plot* or *a simple plot* and about how *a plot develops*.

Answers

1. c.   2. a.   3. d.   4. b.   5. f.   6. h.   7. e.   8. g.

4 Other kinds of feelings

In this exercise, students practise ways of turning down suggestions. Lead in by asking the class to imagine they have a friend who is depressed, upset or stressed-out. They should come up with suggestions to cheer their friend up. Elicit different structures for making suggestions and write them on the board. For example:
Why don't we … ?
How about … ?

Then elicit different ways in which their friend could politely turn down the suggestions. Explain that this exercise will present another way of making suggestions to do something together, as well as several ways to turn a suggestion down.

Have students complete the matching task and then play the recording so they can check their answers. Play the recording again and stop after each line so students can repeat the sentence.

After students have underlined the expressions, they can practise the conversations in pairs. To help students say the phrases fluently, use this method: one person looks at the first suggestion and memorises it. Then they look up and say it to their partner without looking at the Coursebook. Their partner does the same with the response. When students have finished, they can swap roles. This also helps them prepare for the next exercise.

Answers

1. b.   2. a.   3. d.   4. c.
The expressions are:
I'm not really in the mood
I'd rather just stay in
I've been on my feet all day
I can't be bothered
It'll take ages to get there

You may need to explain a few of these expressions:

- If you are *not in the mood for something*, you don't feel like doing it.

- If you say *you've been on your feet all day*, you have been very busy and haven't had a chance to sit down and relax.

- If you *can't be bothered (to do something)*, you don't want to make the effort to do it. Refer students to the **Real English** note.

Also, point out the pattern *Do you fancy + -ing?*

5 Free practice

Students can now practise having conversations similar to those in **4 Other kinds of feelings**. Encourage them to continue the conversation a little more. Give an example before they start:

A: *Do you fancy getting something to eat?*

B: *I don't feel like it. I'm not hungry.*

A: *Well, how about a drink?*

B: *I can't be bothered. Can't we just stay in and watch TV?*

Follow up by having students go around making their own suggestions to different members of the class.

Using grammar

1 Two uses of the present continuous

Students may have learned that the present continuous is used to describe actions that are happening now. Although the tense can be used in this way, it does not always hold true. When it refers to the present, it is perhaps better to think of the present continuous as describing an unfinished action.

Explain the situation and talk about how the expression *bump into* is used to say that the two people met by chance. Play the recording and ask students to listen for the answers to the two questions. Then find the examples of the present continuous in the tapescript on page 149.

Let students read the explanations of the two uses and decide which examples from the conversation fit which category. They can then compare their answers with a partner before checking with you. You might need to explain that if you *pick up* a friend, you meet them somewhere and then drive them in your car, and that if something happens *out of the blue*, it happens unexpectedly.

Answers

1. They're on holiday, but are stuck inside somewhere, perhaps a shopping mall, because it's raining.

2. Lauren is fed up with all the rain. She is frustrated because she wanted to get some sun. Ben feels the same way.

Examples of the present continuous:

1. How's it going?
2. So, what're you doing here?
3. Are you doing some shopping or something?
4. I'm just having a wander around.
5. My wife's waiting for me.
6. We're actually going to the market now.

2 Practice

In this exercise, students apply the rules from the previous exercise to determine which function of the present continuous is being expressed. After they have finished, have them explain their answers with a partner. They should come to the conclusion that the examples referring to the future have a time phrase *(later, in the summer, tonight, at nine o'clock tomorrow morning)*. Ask them to go back and underline these phrases. Then have them practise telling each other about their plans for the week. You could also teach them the expression *I'm not doing anything special* after they've finished.

Answers

1. b. 2. a. 3. b. 4. a. 5. b. 6. b. 7. a. 8. a.
9. b. 10. a.

You may need to explain the following expressions:

- If you *do overtime*, you work and are paid for hours that exceed your regular work schedule.

- A *shift* is a set period that employees work before being replaced by another group. For example: *do an extra shift, work the night shift, I hate working shifts.*

- If you *cover for someone*, you do their job for them because they aren't at work.

- If *it's pouring with rain*, the rain is heavy.

3 Questions and answers

Students should match the questions 1–7 to the appropriate answers a–g. While going through the answers, model the pronunciation of the questions, focusing on the intonation and stress. Have students repeat after you until they feel comfortable saying the expressions. Pairs of students can then practise the questions and answers themselves. You may need to explain the following expressions:

- If you *go window shopping*, you just look at the goods displayed in the shop windows from the street and you don't go into the shops to buy anything. Ask students what the equivalent in their language is.

- If you *give something up*, you stop doing it. For example: *I've decided to give up smoking. I gave up waiting and went without him.*

- If you *do temping*, you don't work as a full-time permanent employee for a company. You usually work for a temping agency and work for a short time in one place before moving on to another place.

Answers

1. c. 2. b. 3. e. 4. a. 5. g. 6. d. 7. f.

4 Further practice

Get students to work in pairs with these conversations. Encourage them to add a follow-up comment like the example.

5 Free practice

Refer students to the photographs. Check that they know what the places are and then practise the example with a student. You could use this to recycle some of the language from the previous exercises by adding more to the conversation. For example:

A: *Hi, Nick. How's it going?*

B: *Not bad. I'm a little tired. I didn't get much sleep last night.*

A: *So, what are you doing here? Are you going somewhere?*

B: *No, I'm just meeting a friend who's coming to visit. How about you?*

A: *I'm off to spend a few days at my parents'.*

B: *Well, that'll be nice.*

A: *To be honest, it'll be a bit boring. They live in a small village and there's not much to do around there.*

6 Speaking

Use the questions in small groups to reinforce some of the language from **3 Questions and answers** on page 30. Also, take this opportunity to tell students a story about when you bumped into someone or about any experiences you've had doing temp work. Let them listen to you and encourage questions. This is useful input for when they do the task themselves.

7 Negative responses

In this exercise students see how the present continuous can be used to explain why you can't do something. These examples include both present and future meanings. To help students, write some different question starters on the board. For example:

Do you fancy …-ing?

You couldn't … by any chance?

Would you mind … ?

Do you mind if I … ?

I was wondering if you wanted to …

Have you … yet?

As students are working, go around and check how they are doing, helping when necessary. When they have finished, have them practise asking and answering their questions with their partner. Then they should move around the class asking their questions to different people.

> **Answers**
>
> Possible answers:
> 2. Can you fix the toilet?
> 3. Do you fancy coming out for a drink with us after work?
> 4. Have you printed out those documents yet?
> 5. I was wondering if you wanted to go out for dinner with me tonight?
> 6. Do you fancy coming round to my place for a romantic dinner?
> 7. Can I see if the news is on?
> 8. Can I turn that down?

Explain that if you are *seeing* someone, you are dating/going out with them. You could also ask *Are you seeing anyone at the moment?*

Follow-up

Have pairs of students write a television interview with Jim and Andrea. They should include both the questions and the couple's answers. The only rule that you should give is that they must include at least eight adjective + noun collocations or phrases from **Using vocabulary** on page 28. This activity would work best in groups of three, as students can then role-play the interview to the class or to other groups.

Review: Units 1-4

The review exercises can be used as a test. However, **4 Look back and check** and **8 What can you remember?** are better done as a discussion in pairs.

1 Tenses

Answers

1. a. 'm doing b. 'm really enjoying c. started
    d. missed e. 've only been doing

2. a. Have you ever been b. went c. was
    d. was travelling e. met f. Are you thinking

3. a. are you doing b. 'm meeting c. 're having
    d. 'm really looking forward to
    e. 've been planning f. haven't had

2 Grammar review

Answers

1. when	5. have you been	9. I'm meeting
2. boring	6. I'm using	10. since
3. going	7. I was living	
4. for	8. did you do	

3 Word order

Answers

1. A: Have you ever been to Brazil?
    B: No, I've never been anywhere in South America.
2. No, I haven't finished writing this yet.
3. Yeah, I've just seen her in the coffee bar.
4. No, I've already seen it, I'm afraid.
5. I can't believe you've never been abroad!
6. I don't know. I've always been into it, I suppose.

4 Look back and check

Answers will vary.

5 Verb collocations

Answers

1. j. 2. h. 3. a. 4. d. 5. b. 6. i. 7. c. 8. g.
9. f. 10. e.

6 Adjectives

Answers

1. pregnant	5. annoying	9. awful
2. boring	6. scary	10. sunburnt
3. strong	7. interesting	
4. great	8. stressful	

7 Questions and answers

Answers

1. f. 2. b. 3. h. 4. d. 5. e. 6. a. 7. j. 8. g.
9. c. 10. i.

8 What can you remember?

Answers will vary.

9 Common expressions

Answers

1. given 2. makes 3. mood 4. fancy 5. wouldn't
6. give 7. took 8. grew 9. exactly 10. fan

Answers for 11–14 will vary.

10 Revision quiz

Answers

1. Possible answers: How old are you? How much do you earn? Are you married?

2. Do you have any brothers or sisters?

3. Words that are commonly used together.

4. Tidy it up.

5. Possible answers: took it easy, read a book, did my homework.

6. Possible answers: the cinema, church, a club.

7. Possible answers: a bridge club, a tennis club, a chess club.

8. Possible answers: book a flight, rent a cottage, hire a car.

9. In a tent.

10. Because they include everything for a low price.

11. *It's great* means you know that it's wonderful. *It's supposed to be great* means that you've heard from someone else that it's wonderful.

12. In a rucksack/backpack.

13. Possible answers: I didn't get much sleep, I worked late.

14. Possible answers: it's been raining all week, work is stressful.

15. Possible answers: *EastEnders* and *Coronation Street*.

16. You haven't paid your rent for a while.

17. You take them somewhere in your car.

18. In a swimming pool or in the ocean.

19. Possible answers: stamps, coins, phone numbers.

20. Possible answer: It's sometimes difficult to remember the grammar rules and vocabulary.

5 Work

Unit overview

General topic
Talking about work.

Dialogue
Maria and Ken talk about what their jobs involve.

Language input

- Expressions to talk about work: *I work part-time. I used to work for a dotcom company. I work as a sales assistant.* etc.

- Using *have to, don't have to* and *can*: *I have to travel a lot. I don't have to work at weekends if I don't want to. I can wear what I like to work.*

- Expressions with *get used to* and *be used to*: *I'll never get used to it. I'm so used to getting up early.* etc.

- Expressions with *get to*: *I get to travel a lot.* etc.

- Expressions with *must*: *You must get a bit depressed. That must be good.* etc.

Language strip

Use the language strip as a way to lead in to the unit. Ask students to quickly look through the list and find any expressions that would be true for them now (e.g. *I'm in computers*) and any expressions that they would like to be true for them in the future (e.g. *I've just got a rise*). Explain that in this unit they will learn ways to talk about jobs. Encourage them to choose some other expressions in the strip that look interesting and to find out more about them.

Use the language strip later on in this unit for a small group task. Ask students to find those expressions that use the present perfect (e.g. *How long have you been out of work?*) and those that use the present continuous (*I'm thinking of leaving my job*). You could also think about how to answer the expressions that are questions. For example:
A: *What's the pay like?*
B: *Not bad.*

You might need to explain some of the following expressions:

- If you are *out of work*, you don't have a job. For example: *I've been out of work since I left school.*

- A *traffic warden* is someone who controls parking on the streets and issues parking tickets.

- If you *work on an assembly line*, you work in a factory doing a particular job in the manufacturing process. You do your work on the product before it continues down the line to the next person. Cars are built on assembly lines.

- If you say *I'm in computers*, your job involves computers. If you are *into computers*, computing is your hobby. You can also say *I'm in real estate/business/banking*, etc.

- If you are *sacked*, you lose your job because your work or behaviour has not been good. For example: *He's always falling asleep on the job. I'm surprised he hasn't been sacked yet.*

- If you *get a rise*, you get an increase in your pay. For example: *I've just heard we're not getting a rise this year.*

- If you *go freelance*, you start to work independently and get paid by different companies who buy your work. For example: *freelance photographer, freelance writer*.

Remind students to record any of the expressions that they like in their notebooks.

Lead in

Have the class tell you how one could ask about someone's job in English. For example:
What do you do?
What do you do for a living?
Where do you work? etc.

Write the expressions on the board and then ask each student to think of five ways of answering these kinds of questions with jobs that they wished they had. Then get students into pairs and ask them to talk about the jobs they chose and why they chose them.

Using vocabulary

1 What do you do?

Draw students' attention to the pictures and have them work in pairs making guesses about the people's jobs. You might have to explain that *I reckon* is an informal way of saying *I think*. Encourage them to explain their choices. Point out the expression *or something (like that)*, which is added to emphasise that we aren't sure. Then play the recording so students can listen and check if they were right. Write these expressions on the board so students can tell you where their guesses were different:
I thought he/she was a … but he/she's actually a …
I thought he/she was a … but it turns out he/she's a …

Play the recording a second time while students fill in the gaps. After checking the answers, write these patterns on the board:
I work as a …
I work for/in a …
I work for/in a … as a …

Ask students to make some more sentences using these patterns. You might need to explain that you work in a place/town/city, but you work for a company/an organisation. Point out other useful phrases to talk about your job: *I'm self-employed, once I graduate, work part-time.* Explain that a dotcom company is a company that does most of its business on the Internet. A lot of dotcoms went bankrupt in 2000.

Answers

1. a painter and decorator
2. a graphic designer
3. a designer
4. in a bank
5. work part-time
6. a waitress
7. a local school
8. a computer programmer

---

2 Free practice

Introduce this task by talking about yourself, what you used to do, and any members of your family. Try to use some of the structures from **1 What do you do?** and encourage students to ask you questions. Note that some students might not want to talk about what their parents do for a living or might not know exactly how to describe their job. Give them general expressions like the following.
She works in business.
She runs her own business.

3 Speaking

Have students work in small groups to discuss these questions, and then have them report back their ideas to the whole class. This is a good opportunity for students to talk about how the Internet has and hasn't revolutionised the way we live and work, the problems of unemployment, and the issue of working parents. You may want to add further questions on any of these topics if your students seem interested in talking more about them.

4 Do you like it?

This task introduces the verbs *have to, don't have to* and *can* in the context of talking about work. The examples will help students to form a rule to help them use these verbs.

As a lead-in, get students in pairs to list the good things and bad things about some of the jobs in the pictures on page 36. For example, a waitress can get free food but she probably doesn't make a lot; a teacher has to do a lot of work in the evenings, but it's probably very rewarding.

Have students work individually before comparing their ideas with a partner. As you go through the answers, ask them to suggest what job they think the person has, for

example, the person in number 3 might work in a fast food restaurant.

Answers

The sentences where the person likes their job are: 2, 4, 5, 7, 10, 11 and 14.
The sentences where the person doesn't like their job are: 1, 3, 6, 8, 9, 12 and 13.

Remind students to underline complete expressions when they go back and find uses of *have to, don't have to* and *can* (e.g. *I often have to work late*). Ask students if they notice any pattern, and then complete the rules a. and b. that follow in the next task for them. Go over the explanation in the Coursebook and answer any questions.

Answers

a. have to   b. don't have to, can

Students can then apply the rule to the last task. Again, as you check their answers, ask what kind of job the person is talking about.

Answers

15. have to	19. have to	23. don't have to
16. don't have to	20. can	24. can
17. have to	21. don't have to	
18. have to	22. can	

Point out the following patterns and encourage students to record them in their notebooks along with a couple of examples:
I don't have to … if I don't want to.
I can … if I want to.
I don't have to … . It depends if I feel like it or not.
I can … what/where/when I like.

This exercise contains many useful expressions for talking about work. Give students a few minutes to go back and underline those they find interesting and to record them in their notebooks.

Real English

Refer students to the **Real English** note. Ask them to think of instances when they might use the expression *Thank goodness.* Has anything happened to them recently that made them happy? Do they remember a time when they were greatly relieved?

5 Free practice

Let students spend a minute thinking about what the job they have chosen involves. Then model and practise the phrases, noting how *have to* is pronounced /hæv tə/. If students guess quickly, they can repeat the exercise, but with different jobs.

Using grammar

1 A good job

Discuss what accounting involves before asking students if it sounds like an interesting job. Have them talk about what an accountant has to do, what the pay and hours are like. Then have them read the text and share their reactions with a partner.

You might want to talk about the expression *push you into*. Ask students whether their parents ever pushed them into something. Also, point out the expression *job security*. Ask what other kinds of jobs provide good job security. You may need to explain that if something *drives you mad*, it annoys you and that if a report is *dry* it is not interesting.

2 Get used to/be used to

This section focuses on the expressions *get used to* and *be used to*. Go over the explanation in the Coursebook with the class, pointing out that *I'm used to* and *I've got used to* both mean that you now see a situation as normal, while *I'm getting used to* or *I'm trying to get used to* both mean you don't feel totally comfortable about a situation yet. Point out that these expressions are followed by a noun or quite often an *-ing* form. You may also need to discuss the difference between these expressions and *used to*, as in *I used to do karate when I was younger*.

Before students tell their partners what they could *get used to/never get used to*, complete two examples for the class:
I could never get used to working nine to five because I've worked as a teacher for so long.
I think I could get used to being self-employed because I'd like to be my own boss.

Ask a few students to share some of their sentences with the class.

3 Matching

This exercise provides students with several typical patterns with *get/be used to*. After students have finished the matching task, tell them to go back and underline the complete expressions. Encourage the students to record these in their notebooks. Model and practise the pronunciation of the expressions in the Coursebook as you go through the answers. You also might want to ask some further questions to practise using some of the other expressions here. For example:
Does anyone here find it difficult to get up early?
How long would it take you to get used to working nights?
Would you find it difficult to work from home?
Do you know anyone who works a six-day week?

Answers

I. e.   2. d.   3. a.   4. b.   5. c.   6. f.

4 Speaking

Here, students use the expressions from **3 Matching** to talk about how comfortable they feel about different aspects of English. Remind them that if any of the sentences are not true for them, they should choose another expression that will make it true (e.g. *I'm still trying to get used to the different sounds of English*). This is a chance for you to review some of these aspects and reinforce some of the learning advice from the first unit.

5 Word order

This exercise further helps to reinforce the *get used to* and *be used to* expressions. Have students first work individually, and then have them practise reading the conversations in pairs. Draw attention to the two patterns in the following questions:
How are you finding … ?
How do you find … ?

Explain that the present continuous form is often used when a situation is new or temporary whereas the present simple is typically used when the situation is more established.

Answers

1. still haven't got used to
2. slowly getting used to
3. just get used to it
4. don't think I'll ever get used to
5. took me a long time to get used to
6. sure I'll get used to

Real English

Refer students to the **Real English** note. Ask if they would like to work behind a desk all day. Tell students about times when you were stuck: at a job, in traffic, etc. Ask them if they've ever felt this way and what they did about it.

6 Role play

Before students do this role play, talk about a time when you, or someone you know, went abroad. Tell them how you found the things listed here and how quickly you got used to or didn't get used to them. You might want to have students do the role play twice with different partners so that they can improve their performance.

Listening

1 Before you listen

Explain the situation of the dialogue and have students work in pairs discussing what Maria's and Ken's jobs might be. Remind them of the structures *work for/as/in…* .

2 While you listen (So, what do you do?)

Tell students to listen for the answers to the two questions. Play the recording, making sure that students cover the text. Get them to discuss their answers in pairs. Remind students to keep the text covered as they do this.

Answers

1. Maria is a drugs worker and Ken works for Barclays Bank.
2. Maria's job involves going out in a van, distributing food and clean needles to drug addicts. She also helps them find a doctor or gets them into a rehabilitation centre if necessary. Ken's job involves buying and selling currency. He gets to travel quite often to New York.

Words in gaps in the conversation:
1. involve
2. drug addicts
3. healthy
4. find a place
5. Not at all
6. spread diseases
7. very rewarding
8. don't have to
9. Doing what?
10. have to work
11. get to travel

Next, let students read the dialogue as you play the recording again. Then ask them, in pairs, to fill in the first two or three gaps from memory before you play the recording again, this time with pauses so that they can check and fill in the missing words. Do this two or three gaps at a time until the end. Play the recording through one more time with students following the text. If you want students to read the conversation, or parts of it, in pairs, use the tapescript on page 150. (The missing words are in colour.)

Students might ask you about the following expressions:

- If you say *someone doesn't want to know you*, they don't want to be in contact or have any kind of relationship with you. For example: *Ever since we had that little disagreement over the coffee money, he hasn't wanted to know me.*

- If you try not to *make judgements*, you try not to express your personal opinion about whether something is right or wrong. For example: *It's important for social workers not to make judgements about the people they are working with.*

- You use *but then again* to talk about a positive aspect of something after you have mentioned a negative aspect, or vice versa. For example: *Ibiza is very touristy, but then again, it's cheap.*

Real English

Refer students to the **Real English** note on *get to* and have them use this structure to talk about themselves. You could use the pictures of different jobs on pages 36 and 37 to ask students for further examples:
A postman gets to be outside a lot.
A nurse gets to meet lots of people.
etc.

3 Speaking

Students can either discuss the questions in this exercise in small groups, or the class could debate. Divide the class into two groups: one in favour of Maria's approach, the other against. Give students five to ten minutes to brainstorm reasons to support their point of view, and then get them into small groups of four, two from each side, to argue in support of their position. You could also do this with the question about money being the most important thing about a job.

4 Opinions with *must*

Must is often used when we imagine what a situation is like based on what someone has just said. When used in this way, it often serves as a means of empathising with the other speaker.

Let students read the two extracts from the conversation and underline the two examples of *must*, and then go over the explanation.

Answers

The two expressions with *must* are:
You must get a bit depressed
That must be good

Encourage students to write the patterns *that must be +* adjective and *you must get +* adjective in their notebooks. You could also point out that *you must get* can be followed by *-ed* forms of adjectives while *that must be* can be followed by *-ing* forms. For example:
You must get depressed/frustrated/bored, etc.
That must be depressing/interesting/frustrating/worrying, etc.

Let students work individually or in pairs to complete the dialogues. Remind them to add an appropriate response as well. Play the recording so that they can check their answers. Then discuss what jobs the people are talking about.

Answers

1. That must be
   Possible response: Yeah, it is/can be.
   Possible job: any job that involves commuting

2. You must get
   Possible response: Yeah, I do (sometimes).
   Possible job: a security guard

3. That must be
   Possible response: Yeah, it is/can be.
   Possible job: a traffic warden

4. That must be
   Possible response: Yeah, it is/can be.
   Possible job: an English teacher

5. You must get
   Possible response: Yeah, I do (sometimes).
   Possible job: a nurse

6. You must get
   Possible response: Yeah, I do (sometimes).
   Possible job: an accountant

5 Pronunciation: sentence stress

Play the recording once all the way through with students listening. Ask them to pay attention to how the stressed words sound. Then play the recording again, pausing after each sentence to allow students to repeat. Practise these sentences until students can say them naturally.

Finally, get them to practise the conversations in **4 Opinions with *must*** in pairs, with the appropriate stress. You may want to point out that when *quite* is stressed (*quite* tired), it means *not too (tired)*, but when the adjective following *quite* is stressed (quite *tired*), it means *very (tired)*.

6 Further practice

Ask students to get into pairs and have short conversations based on these openings. As they converse, encourage them to keep the conversation going. You may make suggestions as you monitor students' progress.

Alternatively, you can write the sentences in the Coursebook on slips of paper and give one to each student. They should then find another student, say the sentence on their slip and continue the conversation. Then the other person does the same. When students have finished, they exchange slips and find another person, repeating the procedure with the sentence on their former partner's slip.

Follow-up

As an extension of this unit, put students into pairs to design a recruitment campaign for a particular job. Remind them of the following useful patterns.
You'll get to …
You can … if you want to.
You don't have to … if you don't want to.
You'll quickly get used to …

Give students time to go back through the unit to find additional expressions for this project. Once groups are finished, ask that they present their campaign to the class. You can finish up by having the class vote on which group had the most appealing job. Alternatively, you could set this as a writing task.

Unit overview

General topic
Places to buy things.

Reading
Why car-boot sales are better than global chains.

Language input

- Expressions with *thing*: *I've got to pack my things tonight. That was a stupid thing to do!* etc.
- Collocations for things you buy: *a great pair of jeans, a lovely bunch of flowers,* etc.
- Vocabulary for different kinds of shop: *a newsagent's, a chemist's,* etc.
- Asking for and giving directions: *Is there a garage near here? There's one five minutes' drive down the road.* etc.
- Agreeing: *So do I. Neither do I.*
- Collocations with money: *I earn four hundred pounds a week plus overtime. I was left ten thousand pounds when my aunt died.* etc.
- Expressions with *must, mustn't, have to* and *don't have to: I must remember, I mustn't forget, We have to be at the hotel by 9:30, I'm glad I don't have to,* etc.

Language strip

Use the language strip as a way to lead in to the unit. Ask students to look quickly through the list and find any expressions that they have used themselves while shopping. Explain that in this unit they will learn other ways to talk about places to shop and about using money. Encourage them to choose some other expressions in the strip that look interesting and to find out more about them.

Use the language strip later on in this unit for a small group task. Ask students to find expressions in the list that might be said to a shop assistant (e.g. *Can I try it on?*) and those that might be said to a friend (e.g. *Where did you get it?*). You could also ask them to underline all the expressions that use *get*.

You might need to explain some of the following expressions:

- *I think I'm a small, Have you got it in medium?* and *I'm a nine* all refer to sizes in clothing.
- *Shop till you drop* is an expression suggesting that you are going to do a lot of shopping. For example: *Let's go into town and shop till we drop!*

- If you describe something as *cheap and cheerful*, you mean it is not expensive but still looks all right. For example: *When it comes to dishes, I'd rather have cheap and cheerful than expensive.*
- If you say *I wouldn't be seen dead doing something*, you mean you would never do it because you dislike it so much. For example: *I wouldn't be seen dead wearing a Gap skirt.*
- A cashier might say *Have you got the 15p?* if the total came to £8.15, for example, so that you don't end up with a lot of change.
- If something is *not really you*, it doesn't really suit you. For example:
  A: *My mother sent me this jacket. What do you think?*
  B: *Well, it's not really you.*
- *Benetton* and *Gap* are clothing chains; *Amex* is *American Express.*

Remind students to record any of the expressions that they like in their notebooks.

Lead in

Ask students whether they like shopping, how much time they spend shopping, and where they go shopping. Discuss whether they see shopping as a pastime or as a necessity, and explain the difference between *I did the shopping* and *I went shopping.*

Reading

1 Speaking

This task focuses on different places to shop and helps lead in to the reading task. Draw students' attention to the pictures. Have them match the places to the pictures and briefly answer any questions. The topic of the reading text is car-boot sales, so you don't need to go into much detail if students ask about this.

Answers
1. d   2. b   3. e   4. a   5. f   6. c

After checking their answers, put students in pairs and get them to talk about each place using the sentence starters. Note that it is also possible to omit the words *the fact*:
One good thing about shopping in … is that … .

When students discuss questions 7 and 8, write these phrases on the board:
I'd never go to … because …
I wouldn't be seen dead in a place like that!

You may need to explain the difference between *I'd never go* and *I've never been*. Ask which one is indirectly expressing an opinion (*I'd never go*).

2 While you read (I'm a car-boot sale addict and proud of it!)

Go over the questions in the Coursebook with students before they read the article. Then ask them to read the article and discuss their answers and their overall reactions with a partner. Encourage them to use expressions from the text.

Answers

1. The author enjoys car-boot sales because you can find different and unusual things there and sometimes pick up amazing bargains.
2. The author hates global chains because there is nothing surprising about them. They are dull and predictable. The prices are also high.

Play the recording of the article as students follow along in their Coursebooks. Ask them to underline any expressions or collocations that interest them. Offer to explain any words or expressions that they are unsure of. Here are some expressions to do with shopping or business that you might want to point out:

corner the market
go out of business
go bankrupt
old junk
make up prices on the spot
pick up amazing bargains
haggle over prices
bits and pieces
being ripped-off
big business

Tell students to add the expressions they like to their notebooks.

Real English

Refer students to the **Real English** note. Do they ever receive *junk mail*? What do they do with it? Do they have some old junk they'd like to get rid of?

3 Speaking

Students can discuss these questions in small groups. Before they start, give them some sentence starters to help them talk about what they agree and disagree with in the article:

One thing I agree/disagree with is …

I don't really agree when the author says …

Personally, I think/don't think …

The author has a point when she says …

I don't think that's totally true …

4 Thing – an important word in English

Although English speakers use this word frequently, you can point out that it is also useful when learners of English don't know the words for something. Introduce some examples they could use:

What's that thing you use to get ice cream out of a carton?

What do you call that thing you stand on and weigh yourself with?

What's the name of the thing over there?

You could even turn this into a little game with students testing each other on the names of objects in English.

When students have finished talking about unusual or interesting things, get them to do the matching task and check their answers with a partner. Point out that they are choosing something that *thing(s)* might be referring to, not what it always refers to when it is used like this. Explain that *trunks* are what men wear when they swim. Encourage students to record these expressions in their notebooks, perhaps on a page just for *thing* expressions.

Answers

1. b.   2. c.   3. a.   4. h.   5. f.   6. d.   7. g.   8. e.

Follow up by discussing other examples of what *thing* could refer to in numbers 3–8 and explain that *thing* doesn't only refer to objects.

The next task presents another common English expression using the word *thing* in an abstract sense. Share one of the stupidest things you have ever done with the class before students work on their own stories. Here is a model:

Well, what happened was I was over at my grandfather's old house – he had died a few weeks before – helping sort out some of his old things. I was only about fifteen and most of it just looked like junk to me. Anyway, there was a knock at the door, and it was some man asking for donations to a jumble sale. I invited him in and said he could take whatever he wanted. He ended up taking quite a bit of stuff. It was only when my parents came over to collect the priceless antiques my grandfather had collected that I realised what I'd done and that I needed to leave the country as soon as possible!

You could also give students alternatives like *the bravest/funniest/strangest thing* if they are having problems thinking of ideas. When they have finished, ask them to tell the same story to a different partner. Finish up with the discussion questions.

As an extension, have pairs of students role-play a dialogue at a car-boot sale. Introduce some expressions for haggling. For example:

How much do you want for this?
That's a bit expensive, isn't it?
I'll give you five pounds for it.
Five pounds? You must be joking!
It's worth a lot more than that.
You can have it for a pound.

Alternatively, use the pictures to practise using *thing* for unknown objects. Ask pairs of students to talk about what they think the objects are. This is also a good opportunity to talk about spatial position. For example:

What do you think that thing over there is?

This thing?
The thing next to it.
What do you use this thing for?
Where did you get that thing?
That's the strangest/weirdest/most unusual/ugliest/most beautiful thing I've ever seen. What is it?

5 Matching

This exercise focuses on several useful collocations connected with things we buy. Once students have matched the parts together to make sentences, go over the pronunciation and have them memorise the expressions. Pairs of students can then test each other, with one student reading the first part aloud and the other student completing the sentence without looking at the Coursebook. They can then swap roles.

> **Answers**
>
> 1. h.   2. d.   3. f.   4. g.   5. e.   6. a.   7. c.   8. b.

After students finish practising the sentences, talk about what you bought on your last shopping trip. Have them listen and ask you questions. Then ask them to recall any collocations you used. For example:

a couple of bottles of cheap red wine
a second-hand copy of 'War and Peace', etc.

Using vocabulary

1 Different shops

Lead in to this task by asking students what they would say to someone in the street if they wanted to find a place to buy a newspaper in Britain. Some suggestions might include:

Where can I buy a newspaper?
Where is the newspaper shop?

Then refer students to the photos on page 44 and have them complete the first conversation. Point out that we often explain what we need and then ask if the place where we can get it is nearby. This is more typical than more direct *where* questions.

After checking their answers, students can practise the conversation in pairs. You might need to explain *nappies* if your students are unfamiliar with this term.

> **Answers**
>
> 1. newsagent's   2. garage   3. chemist's   4. post office
> 5. post box   6. bank   7. restaurant

2 Speaking

Before students practise the conversations with different directions, tell them to go back and underline the direction expressions in **1 Different shops**. Spend a few minutes going over their pronunciation. The direction expressions are:

a couple of hundred metres down the road
opposite the school/park/car park
five minutes' drive down the road
just past the station
on the main road
just down there
just round the corner
outside the newsagent's

For the next task, discuss 1–10 as a class first, supplying any necessary vocabulary for the places (e.g. *photo booth, off-licence, barber's, beauty salon*). Then teach the expression *Is there somewhere near here where I can (send a fax/do some photocopying)?* Pairs of students can then have conversations similar to those in **1 Different shops, 1–7**. Point out the useful verb + noun collocations here (*send a fax, do some photocopying, pick up a prescription*). Finish off with the discussion questions at the end.

3 Matching

This exercise gives students practice with expressions for agreeing: *So do I* and *Neither do I*. Make sure students notice that *So do I* agrees with an affirmative statement and *Neither do I* agrees with a negative one. Note that in the examples here all the verbs are in the present simple. For statements in a tense that uses an auxiliary, for example the perfect and continuous aspects (e.g. *I've never seen …* , *I'm looking for …*), or those with a modal auxiliary or *be* (e.g. *I can't see …* , *I'm not sure*), the auxiliary is used instead of *do* (e.g. *Neither have I, So am I, Neither can I, Neither am I*). However, you can use *Me too* or *Me neither* with all forms.

You may need to explain that *Tesco's* is a British supermarket chain.

Answers

1. e.   2. c.   3. d.   4. a.   5. b.   6. g.   7. f.   8. i.
9. j.   10. h.

4 Speaking

Write some useful expressions on the board before students talk about the questions in the Coursebook. For example:
They've got a good/bad reputation.
Their products are high/low quality.
There's a boycott on …
They're environmentally friendly.

You could extend the discussion by talking some more about brand names and designer labels. Have students list the top brand names in their country for different products and discuss the question of whether you are paying extra for quality or for just the label. Alternatively, ask if there are any boycotts of companies in their country and if so why the companies are being boycotted.

5 Money collocations

Before doing this exercise, write *money* on the board and elicit some verbs that can precede it. Then do the exercise, adding to the list any verbs that students didn't come up with. While going through the answers, practise the pronunciation of these sentences, paying attention to the stress and intonation. Then ask students to make similar sentences that are true for them.

Answers

1. b. iv. (I earn four hundred pounds a week plus overtime.)
2. f. v. (I won a million pounds on the lottery.)
3. c. ii. (I was left ten thousand pounds when my aunt died.)
4. a. iii. (I found a ten-pound note in the street.)
5. d. vi. (I took thirty pounds out of my account this morning and I've spent it all already!)
6. e. i. (I save five pounds a day by taking a packed lunch to work.

Just for fun, see if students can come up with any ridiculous sentences (e.g. *I won seventy three pence on the lottery*). Follow up by discussing the questions at the end of the section in groups or as a class.

Using grammar

1 Must/mustn't

Remind students of expressions with *must* to talk about how we imagine a situation to be (e.g. *That must be good*). In this exercise, students practise two more uses of *must*: to say what we think is important for us to do, and to recommend something. Some students may think that *must* is often used to tell someone what to do. Draw their attention to the fact that *must* is frequently used with *I* and is very much what we personally see as important or necessary. The other use of *must*, as a way of recommending something, (e.g. *You must come and visit*) might not be familiar to some students. Encourage them to record several of the expressions they see in the following exercises in their notebooks.

Go over the examples and explanations with students and answer any questions. Then have them complete 1–10.

Answers

1. must
2. mustn't
3. must
4. must
5. must
6. mustn't
7. mustn't
8. must
9. must
10. must

When you have gone through the answers, point out these phrases: *I must go, I mustn't be late, You must try, I must just go to, I must remember to, I mustn't forget to, You really must, You must come and visit (us) when you come (to Munich)*. Then practise the pronunciation of *must* and *mustn't* in these phrases. Students can then read the conversations in pairs.

2 | Alternatives to *must* and *mustn't*

Here students focus on polite alternatives to *you must*. Again, remind students that *must* is often found with *I*. As you go through the answers, ask further questions focusing on several of the other expressions. For example:

What are some places that don't allow smoking?

Apart from getting tickets, what else can you do in advance? (pay rent, book a hotel)

What can you do when you return home and you have a lot of foreign currency left? (change it back)

When are you expected to pay in cash? When would it be unusual?

Answers

1. c.   2. e.   3. a.   4. d.   5. f.   6. b.

The polite or less direct expressions are:
I'd … if I were you
I'm sorry, … -ing is not allowed
You have to … , I'm afraid
You're not supposed to …

When students have underlined the polite expressions, have them practise the sentences a–f until they feel comfortable saying them.

3 | Speaking

Tell students about your week before asking them to talk about their list. You could teach them the expression *my to-do list*. Again, if you have a story about a time when you forgot something important, tell that to them too.

4 | Speaking

Check that students know what is happening in the pictures before they talk to their partners. Get a few people to share their suggestions with the whole class. You could also brainstorm other situations or annoying habits (e.g. *jumping a queue, smoking in the bathroom*) and come up with polite responses. For the second task, remind students that they can use *must* in expressions like *You must come and visit* or *You must try the squid*.

5 | Focus on *must* and *have to*

Students may wonder about the difference between *have to* and *must*, as many coursebooks treat them as equivalents. Remind students that *must* implies more of a personal obligation while *have to* implies more of an external one. The difference between *don't have to* and *mustn't*, however, will probably be easier for students to see.

6 | Practice

After going through the explanations in **5 Focus on must and have to**, students can apply the guidelines to completing sentences 1–10. You may need to explain that in number 1, *a funny noise* is a strange noise.

Answers

1. must	6. mustn't
2. mustn't	7. have to
3. don't have to	8. must
4. have to	9. don't have to
5. must	10. have to

The person in number 2 is probably the boss. They don't sound rude because bosses can talk down to their employees if they want to. The boss isn't just reporting rules. The boss is saying what they think is very important. It's a threat here!

---

7 | Speaking

Have students discuss the questions in the Coursebook with a partner. Ask them if they would like to share their answers with the class.

8 | Practice

Encourage students to record this pattern along with *Thank goodness I don't have to* from **6 Practice** in their notebooks, along with some of their personalised sentences from this activity. Share some things you're glad you don't have to do with the class. Then use the questions to reinforce some of the other language from **6 Practice**. Ask the class to tell you some other things you can *go around* (e.g. *the shops, old buildings*).

Follow-up

Have students work in pairs, writing a dialogue set in a clothing store. Their dialogue should include several of the expressions from the language strip. Once they have written their dialogue, have them practise it in pairs before they perform it for another group.

7 | Complaints

Unit overview

General topic
Complaining about poor service and annoying people.

Reading
People get things off their chests at Shout_at_us.com.

Language input

- Expressions for making complaints about service and making requests: *I'm sorry, but this coffee isn't very strong. Do you think you could bring me a stronger one, please?* etc.

- Expressions with *had to*: *I had to borrow some from a friend at work. We didn't have to stay till the end.*

- Other ways to express obligation: *strict dress code, compulsory for all students until the age of sixteen, against the law,* etc.

- Expressions for complaining about people: *I can't stand people who … , It drives me mad when people … ,* etc.

Language strip

Use the language strip as a way to lead in to the unit. Ask students to look quickly through the list and find any expressions that they have used themselves or that they have heard other people use. Explain that in this unit they will learn ways to make complaints in English. Encourage them to choose some other expressions in the strip that look interesting and to find out more about them.

Use the language strip later on in this unit for a small group task. Ask students to choose the expressions that might be said in a restaurant. Of these, ask which seem to be polite (e.g. *Excuse me, I ordered the chicken, not the fish*), and which seem to be quite strong (e.g. *I wouldn't feed this to my dog!*). You can also ask them to suggest what is being referred to by *it* or *this* in several of the expressions. For example, in *I'm afraid it's cold, it* might be referring to the soup that someone ordered.

You might need to explain some of the following expressions:

- We often use *can't stand* to say we hate something. *I can't stand people who complain* means *people who complain a lot really annoy me.*

- If someone asks you how something was, and you reply *Don't even ask,* you are implying that it was so bad you don't want to talk about it, although you may actually go on to explain why it was bad. For example:

A: *How was your trip?*
B: *Don't even ask!*

- If you say *I wouldn't feed this to my dog,* you mean that the food is very bad. For example:
Do you call this steak?
I wouldn't feed this to my dog!

- If something is *stale,* it is not fresh, and tastes or smells bad. We usually use it to describe bread, cake or air. It can also be used figuratively with *idea.*

Remind students to record any of the expressions that they like in their notebooks.

Lead in

Brainstorm a list of things that students find annoying, and ask whether they complain about any of them in their own language. Then ask whether they would actually complain directly to the person involved. Ask how they would complain politely in English, and then ask what they would say if they were really angry.

Listening

1 Speaking

Introduce the task by talking about hotels with students. You could also tell them a hotel story yourself. Have them listen and ask you questions. Ask them to recall any useful expressions or interesting collocations and write them on the board. They can then tell a partner their own hotel story. After pairs of students have drawn up their list of problems, have them share their ideas with the class. This is a good way to work on collocations like *bad service, dirty sheets, rude waiters,* etc.

2 While you listen

Explain the situation of the listening text and play the recording. Students can then work in pairs, discussing the questions. Keep them in pairs for the second task. Help with difficulties with meaning when necessary. Then play the recording again so that they can check their answers. You may want to play the recording a third time while students follow the tapescript on page 150. Encourage them to record some of the adjective + noun collocations in their notebooks.

Answers							
1. h.	2. b.	3. e.	4. a.	5. d.	6. c.	7. g.	8. f.

3 Speaking

Students can discuss these questions in pairs. Draw their attention to the pattern used to talk about a hypothetical situation in the past:
I would've/wouldn't have …

Have students practise saying these phrases, paying attention to the contracted form *would've*. You could also use the list of problems in **1 Speaking** to imagine other problems and have students talk about what they *would've/wouldn't have done* if these had happened to them too.

For some extra vocabulary work, ask students to go back and underline examples of phrasal verbs (e.g. *go down to, send back*) and verbs followed by prepositions (e.g. *wait for, speak to, complain about*).

4 Softening complaints

This exercise focuses on how we typically soften our complaints so that we don't offend the person we are complaining to. This might be a good opportunity to discuss the best way to get problems resolved: by being calm, polite but firm, or getting really angry. Go over the examples and explain that structure b. is more polite and that using a positive adjective softens the complaint the most.

As you go through the answers, ask students how to make the complaint with the structure a. or b.

Answers

1. I'm sorry, but this coffee isn't very strong.
2. I'm sorry, but my room is rather cold.
3. I'm sorry, but my room isn't very clean.
4. I'm sorry, but it's rather noisy outside my room.
5. I'm sorry, but my room isn't very cool.
6. I'm sorry, but I've been waiting for rather a long time.
7. I'm sorry, but this chicken isn't very well-done.
8. I'm sorry, but this wine isn't very nice.
9. I'm sorry, but the service has been rather poor.

1. d.   2. a.   3. h.   4. b.   5. f.   6. c.   7. i.   8. g.   9. e.

---

5 Practice

Let students look back at the complaints in **4 Softening complaints**. Then have them close their Coursebooks. Test them by saying *coffee … strong … bring* and get them to respond with *I'm sorry, the coffee isn't very strong. Do you think you could bring me a stronger one?* Check that they are following the appropriate stress and intonation patterns. Continue like this by saying some key words. You may want to write these words on the board to help students remember. Then have them practise the

conversations in pairs. Before they change roles, do an example, with one of the students as A and you as B:

A: *I'm sorry, the coffee isn't very strong. Do you think you could bring me a stronger one?*

B: *Let me see. It tastes fine to me.*

A: *Well, I'd like another one.*

B: *I'm afraid we can't make it any stronger. You can buy another one if you like with an extra shot of espresso.*

Use the pictures of hotels on pages 48 and 49 and get students to discuss in pairs whether they would stay in any of them and explain why/why not. To extend this, have them role-play a conversation between a polite guest complaining about the service and an apologetic hotel manager. Then they can do it again but this time as a very angry guest and a very rude hotel manager.

Using vocabulary

1 Had to

Remind students that *must* implies a personal feeling of obligation while *have to* implies an external obligation. Review the difference between *don't have to* and *mustn't*. Ask students to recall some expressions using these verbs (e.g. *I really must remember to, I mustn't forget to, I'm glad I don't have to*) and then go over the explanation and examples. You could also point out the way *had* is emphasised in the example from the listening text in **2 While you listen** and write this pattern on the board:
… was/were so … I just had to …

Give some examples:
The food was so bad, I just had to leave.
My feet were so tired, I just had to sit down and rest.

Have students come up with other suggestions and practise saying them.

Answers

Gill was talking about the restaurant at the hotel and how awful the service was. They had to 'get out of there and escape' after the chef came out and made Gill's friend, Veronica, cry.

---

2 Practice

In this exercise, draw students' attention to the way *so I had to* is used to give the result of something. Encourage them to record this pattern and several examples in their notebooks. As you go through the answers, point out and talk about some of the other expressions:

- We often use *on my/our/the way to* when giving the background information of where we were going when we are telling a story.

- If you are *short of money*, you don't have enough money on a particular occasion. For example: *Can you lend me a few pounds? I'm a bit short of money this week.* Ask students what they do if they find themselves a little short of money.

- If *a computer crashes*, some program causes an error and the computer shuts down. For example: *That e-mail attachment you sent kept causing my computer to crash, so I had to open it at work.*

Answers

1. f.   2. j.   3. i.   4. a.   5. e.   6. h.   7. c.   8. b.
9. g.   10. d.

To practise the difference between *lend* and *borrow*, write some typical expressions on the board with *lend* or *borrow* gapped out. Get students to supply the appropriate verb. For example:
Could I ... your dictionary for a minute?
Why don't you ... it from the library?
Thanks for ... me your car last night.
Never ... anything to Bob. You'll never get it back.

The memorisation task at the end helps reinforce the patterns as well as several collocations (*pay a bill, start from the beginning, get a taxi, go in to work, spend the afternoon*).

3 Speaking

Introduce this task by telling the class about a personal experience first. If you can't think of one, you could use this as an example:
Well, I didn't have to sleep in a car exactly, more on a main road. I was hitch-hiking through Vietnam, and I'd just got picked up by a car heading south. It was nearly ten o'clock when we suddenly came to a stop. All the other cars had stopped too, and I noticed people had set up tables selling food and drink beside the road. The driver told me I should get something to eat, get out my sleeping bag and sleep on the road. Apparently, the main north-south road closes for the night, so we both had to sleep where we stopped!

Alternatively, give each student a slip of paper and ask them to choose one of the questions here – or make up another one – and write it on the paper. Have them all stand up and go around asking their question to different people.

4 Had to/didn't have to

This is a transformation exercise, but point out the typical phrases and collocations here too. Ask students if they can think of at least one more collocation for these:
have a word with my boss (talk, drink)
get our passports renewed (licence, visa)
e-mail the report (photos, proposal)
stay till the end (the break, speeches)
pay my bill (taxes, babysitter)

Answers

1. had to be at the station by 6:30
2. didn't have to be home early
3. had to have a word with my boss
4. had to get our passports renewed
5. had to get a taxi
6. had to e-mail the report
7. didn't have to stay till the end
8. had to pay my phone bill

---

5 More ways of expressing obligation

This exercise focuses on several expressions that can be used to talk about obligation, or lack of it. When students have finished the matching task, have them underline these expressions.

Answers

1. g.   2. d.   3. a.   4. f.   5. b.   6. c.   7. e.

The expressions are:
a. have military service
b. compulsory (for ... until the age of)
d. conscripted into the army
e. against the law
f. an optional subject
g. strict dress code

---

6 Speaking

This exercise helps reinforce some of the vocabulary from **5 More ways of expressing obligation**. Give students a few minutes to look through the questions before having them discuss in small groups. Finish up by having students close their Coursebooks and try to remember some of the questions to ask you.

7 Excuses

Here students can see a functional use of *had to*. Explain the task and point out the pictures if students need some ideas. Make sure they know expressions like the following:
take/drop off the kids to/at school
babysit the kids
the babysitter didn't show up
have a dentist's appointment

Get pairs of students to complete the sentences and then have them share their excuses with the whole class. Pairs can then practise reading the conversations.

Answers

Possible answers:
1. (Sorry, but I had to) take my kids to school.
2. (Well, I had to) have dinner with my boss.
3. (Sorry, but I had to) take an important business call.
4. (Well, I had to) spend all evening fixing my car.

8 Free practice

Give students time to prepare their story. Encourage them to use some of the expressions from this or previous units. In particular, you may want to review the use of the past continuous to set the background from Unit 1. You could also give them sentence starters like the following:

Did I ever tell you about the time I … ?

One of the most embarrassing/silliest things I've ever done happened while I was …

You thought that was embarrassing/annoying? Wait until you hear about what happened when …

Point out that saying how we felt, as in number 3, is a fairly typical way of ending a story like this. Have students go around telling their story a few times before asking for who had the best story.

Reading

1 While you read (Shout at us.com – The webite that helps you get things off your chest)

Point out the title of the reading text and ask if anyone knows the expression *get things off your chest*. If no one knows, wait until students have finished reading the complaints and ask if they can guess the meaning. (If you *get something off your chest*, you talk about something that has been worrying or annoying you, in order to help you feel better.)

Ask students whether they tend to *get things off their chest* or *bottle things up*. Have them discuss their reactions in pairs. As a class, find out which complaints most people agree or disagree with. Then play the recording while students follow along in their Coursebooks. Have them underline any expressions they find interesting. Point out the expressions with *must* in the first complaint (*We must have lunch sometime, We must get together*). You may need to explain some of these expressions:

- If you say someone or something is *weird*, you think he/she/it is strange. For example: *Don't you think it's weird how she always knows what you're thinking?*

- If you say something or someone is *sick*, you think he/she/it is disgusting or morally wrong. For example: *It's sick the way they experiment on animals.* You can

also say *I'm sick and tired of something* when you are fed up with it. Refer students to the **Real English** note on *sick and tired*.

- *B.O.* is an abbreviation for *body odour*.

- If you tell someone to *mind their own business*, you rudely tell them not to ask or talk about something you think is private. For example: *I don't see that it's anything to do with you. You should mind your own business.*

2 Speaking

Go over the sentence starters, practising the pronunciation before having students work in pairs. If they are having trouble, give them a model: *I can't stand people who throw litter on the street.*

Point out another structure for complaining in the reading text: *I hate the way …*

You could also teach the expression *I hate it when people … .*

You might need to explain the difference between *I can't stand people who …* (which means *I hate people who …*) and *I don't understand people who …* (which means *I find people who … very strange*).

As an extension, have pairs of students come up with responses to some of the complaints in the reading text that they disagree with. For Shane's complaint, for example, they could come up with responses like *Most accidents are caused by young people, older drivers are just driving carefully*, etc.

3 Problems

One way to do this exercise is to have students listen to the recording first with their Coursebooks closed. Ask them to tell you where they think each situation is taking place. Then play the recording a second time as they fill in the gaps.

Pairs of students can then practise the conversations. Ask if anyone has experienced any of these situations in an English-speaking country. Ask if they complained and if they can remember what they said.

Tell students to go back and underline the expressions for apologising and talking about the problem. Have them record these in their notebooks along with an appropriate translation.

Answers

1. 1. I'm afraid   2. bring me some more   3. without
2. 1. I think I gave you   2. I'm sorry, but
3. 1. Did you say   2. must be

4 Speaking

Once students have practised these conversations, have them change partners and do the exercise again, but this time change one aspect of the problem, a chicken instead of an egg salad sandwich, for example. Then discuss as a class the question at the end. You could teach the verb *short-change*.

You might want to introduce other questions that involve moral decisions. For example:
If you found £5, would you keep it? How about £10? £100?

Would you say anything if you discovered that your pay check had been deposited twice into your account?

5 Role play

Explain the two situations. Then give students a few minutes to go back and look over the language in the unit. As they are writing the dialogues, go around helping when necessary. Once they've practised saying the dialogues, have pairs of students perform them to another pair or to the rest of the class.

Follow-up

One way to round off this unit is to go back to the language strip and have groups of three students write a dialogue between two diners and the waiter/manager. They should try to use several of the expressions in the language strip. They can then rehearse it a few times until they feel comfortable. Finally, have them perform their skit in front of the class.

8 House and home

Unit overview

General topic
Talking about where you live and who you live with.

Reading
Two brothers in their mid-thirties still share a room in their parents' house.

Language input

- Vocabulary to describe different kinds of homes: *studio flat, cottage in the country, detached house*, etc.
- Ways to describe cities and areas: *It's dead. It's a very safe area. It's quite rough.* etc.
- *Always* with the present continuous and *never* with the present simple to complain: *He's always using the phone. She never tidies up after herself.*
- Talking about relationships: *How do you get on with your mum? OK, I suppose. Really well. Not very well.* etc.
- Using *make* and *let* to talk about what you're told to do and allowed to do: *They let you have the weekends off. My parents used to make me eat my greens.*

Language strip

Use the language strip as a way to lead in to the unit. Ask students to look quickly through the list and find any expressions that are true for them and any questions that they could answer affirmatively. Explain that in this unit they will learn ways of talking about where they live and who they live with. Encourage them to choose some other expressions in the strip that look interesting and to find out more about them.

Use the language strip later on in this unit for a small group task. Ask students to think of answers and follow-up comments to some of the questions in the strip. For example:
A: Are you renting?
B: Yes, but I'm thinking of looking for a place to buy.

You might need to explain some of the following expressions:
- *The ground floor* in Britain is *the first floor* in many other countries. It is on the same level as the street.
- In many cities, old warehouses in former industrial areas are being changed into expensive flats. These flats are often called *converted warehouses*.
- You might ask *Have you got mice?* if you think somebody has a problem in their house with rats or mice.

- *Double glazing* is used to describe windows that have two layers of glass, making the house nicer to live in, by keeping the heat in, and wind and noise out.

Remind students to record any of the expressions that they like in their notebooks.

Lead in

As an introduction to this unit, have students brainstorm a list of places to live. These can range from the obvious (e.g. *house, flat*) to the not so obvious (e.g. *Tepee, mansion, caravan, stately home*). Then discuss what advantages and disadvantages students see in living in the more unusual places. For example:
You've got a lot of room in a mansion, but it's probably very expensive to heat.

This leads in nicely to the first exercise.

Reading

1 Different kinds of homes

Focus students' attention on the pictures A–H and have them match them to the descriptions 1–8. This should help explain the meaning of the expressions, but ask the following questions to check, too:
How many main rooms are there in a studio flat?
How many storeys would there have to be for somewhere to be called a big block of flats?
Do you find cottages in the city?
How many floors are there in a bungalow?
Can you think of some examples of slum areas?
Why is it called a detached house?

Have students underline the complete expressions that describe places to live in and add those that they want to remember to their notebooks.

Answers							
1. h	2. c	3. a	4. g	5. e	6. d	7. b	8. f

2 Speaking

This exercise gives students a chance to use some of the expressions in **1 Different kinds of homes**. Have them work in pairs for the first task and then compare their answers with another group. Remind them that there are often several possible answers. They can then talk about the personal reflection questions at the end of the exercise in small groups.

Point out the expression *not very mobile* and ask students to think of situations, apart from being old, in which we could use it about someone (e.g. not having any transportation, having a broken leg). You might also want to talk about how *elderly* is a more polite way of describing someone old.

Answers

Possible answers:
1. best—a ground-floor flat; worst—a huge detached house
2. best—a huge detached house; worst—a tiny little studio
3. best—a run-down place or the tenth floor of a block of flats; worst—a nice cottage in the country
4. best—a studio flat in the city centre, worst—a cottage in the country

---

3 | Speaking

You could start off this task by talking about the first question if your country or generation is different from that of your students'. For the third question, you could divide the class into two groups and have one list the advantages and the other the disadvantages. Go over the pronunciation of the structures before getting students in pairs, one from each group, to talk about their lists.

4 | While you read (Home – but not alone)

Introduce the article and tell students to read it and try and find the answers to the two questions. When they have finished, they can discuss the answers and their overall reaction in pairs. Write some sentence starters on the board to help:
I don't understand why he …
I think it's really bad that …
If I were Dave/Steve, I'd …

Then play the recording of the article while students follow in the Coursebook. Have them underline any expressions or collocations they find interesting. You might want to point out and explain a few yourself.
For example:
a growing number of
I've been in and out of work
have my privacy
drop in and see the kids
prices have rocketed
a rough part of town

Answers

1. Steve is still living at home because he suffers from depression and hasn't been able to keep a steady job. Dave got divorced and left the house to his ex-wife. Neither of them can afford to rent or buy a place in London.
2. They like the fact that they get looked after: get their meals cooked and clothes washed. They also like being with their family. The disadvantages are that they don't have much privacy and Dave finds some of Steve's habits annoying.

---

5 | Speaking

Introduce this speaking task by talking about some of these things yourself. Have students listen and ask you questions. Then ask them if they can recall any useful expressions that you used. Write the expressions on the board to help students while they are discussing these questions themselves.

For the writing task, have the class suggest some expressions that might be useful and write them on the board, making changes to them when necessary. Here are some examples:
The house just felt so empty without them.
They help around the house.
They'll be here to look after us in a few years.
They really need to stand on their own two feet.
I love them, but I wish they'd leave.

Using vocabulary

1 | Cities and areas

Begin by checking that students know the expression *Whereabouts exactly …?* Point out that the present continuous implies that you are talking about a place you don't see as being a permanent residence. You can change it to the present simple if it's more appropriate for your students' situation. Practice the pronunciation and intonation and then have students stand up and ask several people. Remind them to respond or ask a follow-up question too. For example:
A: *Whereabouts exactly are you living?*
B: *In a small flat just down the road.*
A: *Oh, it must be nice, being able to walk to school.*
B: *Yeah, I don't have to worry about getting up so early. So, whereabouts exactly are you living?*

After discussing which students live in the nicest areas, get them in pairs to discuss sentences 1–10, using dictionaries if necessary. They can then use these sentences to describe the pictures on page 56. The matching task reinforces the meaning of the vocabulary.

Answers

The positive descriptions are: 3, 5, 6, 9 and 10.
The negative descriptions are: 1, 2, 4, and 8.
7 could be positive or negative. *Posh* is often used as a slight criticism.

1. e. 2. c. 3. i. 4. f. 5. a. 6. h. 7. j. 8. g.
9. b. 10. d.

Answers

1. He never does anything around the house.
2. She's always leaving her things lying around everywhere.
3. He's always using the phone.
4. He's always leaving the lights on.
5. She never tidies up after herself.
6. She's always leaving her hairs in the bath after she's had a shower.
7. They never let me watch what I want to watch on TV.
8. He's always taking things from my bedroom without asking.
9. He's always interrupting me when I'm talking.

You may need to point out and explain some of the expressions in a–j:

- You can say *a main road runs through somewhere* to say that there is a road in the middle of the area. A river can also be said to *run through* a place. For example: *The Thames runs right through the village.*

- If there is *a lot of prostitution* in an area, it usually means there are women on the street looking for customers to have sex with in exchange for money.

- Ask if there are laws in the students' countries about *clearing up after your dog.* Explain that in Britain a dog's owner is supposed to clear up their dog's excrement from the pavement or street.

For the last task, give students a few minutes to try and remember the expressions a–j. Practise the pronunciation of the example and then have students read the dialogues in pairs. You might want to suggest that they follow up with a comment like *That must be really nice/terrible,* etc.

For the next activity, make sure students know the adjectives listed in the Coursebook. Point out that *disgusting* is fairly strong. Then have pairs of students discuss their answers. There are no absolute answers, although some adjectives like *rude* obviously describe number 9. Point out the expressions *tidy up after yourself* and *take things without asking.*

Answers

Possible answers:
selfish: 3, 7
messy: 2, 5, (6)
disgusting: 6
lazy: 1, (2), (5)
rude: 8, 9
thoughtless: 4 (8)

2 | Further practice

For this task, remind students that the cities listed here are just suggestions. Give some other examples that might be more appropriate for your students if necessary. When they have finished discussing these questions in groups, have them ask you questions about some places that you know.

3 | Always doing/never does

The use of the present continuous with *always* might be strange to some students who may have learned that *always* goes with the present simple. You should explain that it is a fairly common way of complaining about something annoying, especially a habit. When students have finished the rewriting task, go through the answers and ask further questions. For example:
What do you think he should do around the house?
What does 'things' refer to in number 2?
What things should she tidy up?

4 | Pronunciation: sentence stress

Play the recording once all the way through with students listening. Then play it again, pausing after each sentence so students can repeat, following the same stress and intonation pattern.

They can then practise the complaints in **3 Always doing/never does** in pairs. Encourage them to read the sentence to themselves and then look up and say it to their partner. This technique really helps students with the rhythm of English.

5 | Speaking

This exercise gives students an opportunity to use some of the expressions in **3 Always doing/never does**. Write this question on the board:
So, what's it like living at home/sharing a house?

Then have students go around asking others this question and talking about any annoying habits the people they live with may have.

6 How do you get on with them?

This exercise focuses on the expression *get on with* and ways to describe how you get on with someone. Students can complete the conversations 1–4 and check their answers with you. They can then do the same with 5–8. Point out the responses *Really well, Not very well, OK, I suppose*. Practise the pronunciation of these phrases with students before getting pairs to practise reading the conversations. They should then follow up by asking each other how they get along with their mother, father, brothers, sisters, flatmates, classmates, people from work, etc.

You may need to explain the following expressions:

* If you say *we get on like a house on fire*, you mean you have a really good relationship with a person. For example: *We only met yesterday and already we get on like a house on fire.*
* If you are *close to someone*, you like them a lot and know them very well. For example: *I'm very close to my younger sister.*
* If you say *we've got nothing in common*, you mean you don't have the same interests or ideas as the person you are referring to. For example: *It's amazing how little we have in common. You wouldn't believe we're sisters.*
* If you *have a laugh with someone*, you find them fun to be with because you make each other laugh. For example: *It's nice to have a bit of a laugh with your office mates.*

Answers

1. your brother, OK
2. your flatmate, Really well
3. your mum, Not very well
4. your mum, Really well
5. your flatmate, Not very well
6. your brother, Not very well
7. the people you work with, OK
8. the people you work with, Really well

Real English

Refer students to the **Real English** note on *we always have a real laugh*. Have them discuss the questions with a partner. Ask them to tell the class about someone they know who is *a real laugh*.

Listening

1 Speaking

This short reading text leads in to the listening task in **2 While you listen**. Introduce the topic of au pairs, then ask if anyone has been one or has had one in their family. Then have students read the text and share their reaction in pairs. Write some sentence starters on the board:
It sounds like it'd be …
It's probably … but at least you …
I don't think I could ever …

You may need to explain that Exeter is a city in the southwest of England.

2 While you listen

To prepare for the listening task, get students in pairs to predict expressions and collocations containing the words in the box. Have some groups tell you what they have come up with and write them on the board. You can add to or modify them afterwards.

Go over the questions and explain that *the person who wears the trousers* is an expression meaning *the person who tends to make decisions for the family*. Tell students to listen first for the answers to these questions. You may want to have them cover up sentences 1–9. Students can then discuss their answers in pairs.

For the next task, see if students can fill in any of the gaps from memory before you play the recording for them again. Have them record any collocations that are new to them in their notebooks.

Answers

1. Tired.
2. No.
3. Tomorrow morning at seven thirty.
4. Angela. She seems to be the one who makes the decisions.

5. bags 6. coat 7. eat 8. journey 9. show
10. bed 11. alarm clock 12. breakfast 13. show

---

3 Speaking

Ask the first question to the class as a whole before dividing students up into two groups. After they have finished discussing the problems each side face, have pairs of students role-play a dialogue between the au pair and a friend back home after she's been there for a couple of months. Then have them role-play Angela and Paul discussing whether having an au pair is a good idea or not. After students have practised, get pairs to perform one of their dialogues to another group.

4 *Make* and *let*

In this exercise students are introduced to structures with *make* and *let* to talk about things that you are told to do and that you are allowed to do. Let students read the conversation between Katrin and Anna first, and then play the recording as they read and underline the six expressions. Remind them to underline the complete expression. Give students a minute to think about how these expressions are used and what they mean before having them complete sentences 1–10.

Answers

The expressions are:
let you take the morning off
Mine make me work a twelve-hour day
let you have the weekends off
make me take the kids to their ballet classes
let me have friends round for coffee
let me have a little birthday party

1. make 2. let 3. make 4. make 5. let 6. make
7. let 8. let 9. make 10. let

Once you've gone over the answers elicit the two patterns:
(used to) let me + verb
(used to) make me + verb

Point out that the verb is in the base form with no *to* and that *used to* is used to talk about something that is no longer true. Encourage students to record these patterns in their notebooks along with some examples from this exercise or the personalised ones in the next task. Also, point out the expression *take/have the morning/weekends off*. Ask students if they have ever had any days/time off work or off school.

5 Speaking

Here the meaning of the two structures is reinforced. Explain that *authoritarian* is a negative adjective to describe a person who tries to control other people. Point out that it can also be used with *regime, state* or *policy*. For the adjectives in b., explain that they describe someone who is not so strict and allows people more freedom to do things. Ask students if they have ever had any days/time off work or off school.

Answers

1. 1, 2, 3, 4, 6 and 9
2. 5, 7, 8, 10

After going through the answers, have students read through the sentences individually, ticking those that were true for them, and thinking about other things their parents used to let or make them do. They can then talk about this with a partner. You may want to tell them about yourself beforehand or afterwards. Finish up by encouraging students to go back and underline any useful expressions and record them in their notebooks. You may want to point out the following expressions:
stay over at my friend's house
spend the night
go off camping
keep my bedroom neat and tidy
stay up as late as I wanted

6 Role play

This gives students an opportunity to re-use some of the language from this unit, as well as some of the expressions with *have to* and *don't have to* from the previous unit, so give them time to look back through the Coursebook. Explain the situation and give them time to prepare. You could either have them prepare individually, or divide the class into two groups, A and B, and have pairs in each group help each other. Before students start the role play, write a possible opener on the board:
A: *I understand that you have a room to rent.*
B: *That's right. Are you interested?*
A: *Well, I might be.*
Have them do the role play a couple of times with different people. Explain that they will improve their performance each time.

7 Speaking

In this task, students get the chance to be creative. Elicit from them what aspects they should consider and list them on the board, for example, location, size, type of building, number of rooms, special features, etc. You could turn this into a 'real estate activity' by having them draw a picture, set a price and then go around showing it to other students, trying to convince them to buy their dream house.

Follow-up

As a follow-up, tell students to imagine that they have gone to a city abroad to study, and that they've been there for a week. They should write a postcard to one of their friends explaining where they are living, what the city is like and what their flatmates are like. Encourage them to use expressions from this unit. Once they've finished, have them exchange postcards with a partner. They then read each other's postcards before getting together to ask questions about what they read.

Review: Units 5–8

The exercises here can be used as a test. However, **4 Look back and check** and **8 What can you remember?** are better done as a discussion in pairs.

1 Grammar review

Answers

1. I must
2. I mustn't
3. I wouldn't read it if I were you
4. I had to
5. clean
6. make
7. Is it OK if I
8. You must be
9. He's always interrupting
10. get

2 Follow-up comments

Answers

1. d.   2. f.   3. b.   4. c.   5. a.   6. e.

3 Have to, don't have to, can

Answers

1. can
2. don't have to, have to
3. has to
4. don't have to
5. can
6. have to
7. don't have to
8. can
9. aren't allowed to smoke
10. You're not supposed to leave before six.
11. If I were you, I'd phone first to see if they still have tickets left.
12. If I were you, I'd talk to him and see what he says.
13. You aren't allowed in that part of the building.

4 Look back and check

Answers will vary.

5 Verb collocations

Answers

1. a.   2. i.   3. e.   4. j.   5. b.   6. h.   7. c.   8. d.
9. f.   10. g.

6 Adjectives

Answers

1. ignorant   2. wide   3. dead   4. flexible   5. optional
6. strict   7. rewarding   8. latest   9. bright   10. posh

7 Questions and answers

Answers

1. c.   2. f.   3. j.   4. a.   5. h.   6. b.   7. d.   8. e.
9. g.   10. i.

8 What can you remember?

Answers will vary.

9 Common expressions

Answers

1. used   2. something   3. journey   4. wonder
5. common   6. can   7. don't have to   8. mustn't
9. run out of   10. drives

Answers for 11–13 will vary.

10 Revision quiz

Answers

1. *Working shifts* means you work for a certain period of time and then someone else takes over the job. There is no specified time of day in this case. In some jobs – nurses, firefighters – where you work shifts, you work 9–3 one week, 12–9 the next, and so on. *Working nights* means you start work in the evening and finish in the (early) morning.

2. It doesn't fit you.

3. If your car is unreliable, it keeps breaking down. If your friend is unreliable, it means you can't trust or depend on them.

4. Possible answers: bring a packed lunch to work, make your own coffee in the morning, eat at home instead of going to a restaurant.

5. You are really bored.

6. Possible answers: make you come home by a certain time, make you do lots of chores, make you help with the cooking.

7. Possible answers: let you stay up late at night, let you come home whenever you like, let you listen to whatever kind of music you want.

8. You have to do a compulsory subject. You can choose whether to do an optional subject.

9. No. It means that the area is quiet and the nothing is going on.

10. Au pairs live with families and take care of the children.

11. One.

12. You do all the repairs and you redecorate it.

13. Not necessarily. It means that the work gives you satisfaction.

14. Possible answers: school, the hospital, work.

15. Possible answers: phone bill, gas bill, electricity bill, credit card bill.

16. You are.

17. *You're not supposed to* means it isn't allowed. *You don't have to* means that it is not compulsory – but you can do it if you want to.

18. An Internet company.

19. Possible answer: Marks and Spencer/Sogo.

20. Possible answer: Yes, it is. Yes, it can be sometimes.

9 Computers

Unit overview

General topic
Talking about computers and the Internet.

Dialogue
Simon and Pete talk about buying things online.

Reading
Classic computer mistakes.

Language input

- Computer-related vocabulary: *connected to the Internet, check e-mail, my computer crashed,* etc.
- Time expressions: *in a few weeks' time, the other day, all my life, three years ago,* etc.
- Saying e-mail and website addresses: *pete_smith@shotmail.com,* etc.
- Present perfect and past simple: *I bought some grapes this morning. I've eaten them all already.*
- Present perfect with *always* and *never: I've always liked my coffee black. I've never been to South America.*
- Expressions for giving advice: *Why don't you try … ? Have you tried … ? If I were you, I'd …*
- Talking about annoying things with *keep + -ing: I keep having trouble, I keep getting cut off,* etc.

Language strip

Use the language strip as a way to lead in to the unit. Ask students to look quickly through the list and find any expressions that are true for them and any questions that they could answer in the affirmative. Explain that in this unit they will learn more ways of talking about computers and the Internet. Encourage them to choose some other expressions in the strip that look interesting and to find out more about them.

Use the language strip later on in this unit for a small group task. Ask students to think of answers and follow-up comments to some of the questions in the strip. For example:

A: *Know any good sites?*

B: *Yes, one of my favourites is one with all these strange but true stories.*

Other tasks could include finding the expressions that contain the verbs *use (I use Express)* and *get (I get about fifty e-mails a day),* or finding expressions containing phrasal verbs *(Pictures use up so much memory, don't they?).* You might need to explain some of the following expressions:

- *PC* stands for *personal computer* and refers to computers using the Microsoft Windows operating systems, while *Macs* use the Macintosh operating systems.
- *Microsoft Office* is a software suite containing word processing, spreadsheet and other software.
- If you say *I deleted the lot,* you are probably referring to all of the e-mails, files or programs on your computer.
- *Express* is *Outlook Express,* an e-mail software program.
- *AOL* stands for *America Online,* an Internet service provider.
- If you *back something up,* you save a copy of your files, usually in a different location. For example: *Fortunately, I backed up a copy of my work just before the computer crashed.*
- If you *log on,* you enter a name or password to get access to a computer or computer service. For example, you can log on to the Internet/your workstation every morning.
- A *chat room* is a website where people can log on and 'talk' to each other by sending messages from their home computer.

Remind students to record any of the expressions that they like in their notebooks.

Lead in

You can lead in with many kinds of questions about computers. For example:

Do you use computers much?

Do you like using them?

Do you own one?

What's the latest software?

How much time do you spend on the web?

Alternatively, have groups of students brainstorm the areas of life that computers have revolutionised and, more interestingly, the areas they have made more complicated. You can teach the expressions *We couldn't do without them* and *Life was so much easier before.*

Listening

1 Vocabulary

This exercise focuses on computer vocabulary. You could lead in by writing the word *computer* on the board and asking students for some verbs that go before the noun and some that go after. For example:

log off/boot up/shut down/run + computer

computer + crashes/runs slowly/stores information

Tell students that they will see more collocations in the exercise, and that they should underline and record the complete phrases, not just single words, in their notebooks. After they have completed and asked each other the questions, have them close their Coursebooks and see if they can remember the questions to ask you.

Answers

1. PC   2. laptop   3. connected, server   4. software
5. deleted   6. virus   7. check   8. crash

---

2 | Speaking

This exercise helps lead in to the listening task that follows. Have students talk in small groups. You can feed in other questions. For example:
What are some good sites for buying these kinds of things?
Do you ever worry about security?
What are the advantages/disadvantages of buying online?

Tell the class about any personal experiences too before moving on to the next exercise.

3 | While you listen (Recommending a website)

Introduce the listening task and go over the two questions. Tell students to listen for the answers to the questions. Play the recording, making sure that students have covered the text. Get them to discuss the answers in pairs. Tell them to keep the text covered as they do this.

Answers

1. They talk about buying a flight and a CD.
2. Pete wants to book a flight to take Karen away for her birthday. He also wants to buy her a CD with the song that was playing in the bar when they first met as a present.

Next, let students read the conversation as you play the recording again. Then ask students, in pairs, to fill in the first two or three gaps from memory before you play the recording again, this time with pauses so that they can check and fill in the missing words. Do this two or three gaps at a time until the end. Play the recording through one more time, with students following the text. If you want students to read the conversation, or parts of it, in pairs, use the tapescript on page 151. The missing words are highlighted in colour.

Answers

1. why don't you	5. why don't you
2. Have you tried	6. could try looking at
3. if I were you	7. if I were you
4. could try	

For the next task (page 65), ask students first to try remembering the time expressions without referring to the tapescript. They can then look back to check if they were right. Ask the class further questions. For example:
Is anyone going away for the weekend?
Did it rain the other day?
Shall we have a test in a few days' time?

Tell students to record the complete expressions in their notebooks. You may want to point out the following expressions:

- If *you've got access to the Internet,* you can connect to the Internet. You can also use *access* as a verb. For example: *We're always having problems accessing the Internet.*
- If you get *a last-minute deal,* you buy a ticket, for example, a short time before you use it. The price is lower than you would normally pay.
- If a site is *not user-friendly,* people find it hard to use because it is difficult to navigate through or the instructions are confusing.
- *Budget airlines* are airline companies that are able to offer cheaper flights by not providing a lot of the extra services that the regular airlines do. We can also say *budget travel* and *budget-priced CDs* and *hotels.*

Answers

a. Time   b. for   c. other   d. In

---

4 | E-mails and website addresses

Play the recording once all the way through while students just listen, concentrating on how the characters that aren't numbers or letters are said. Then play it again, asking them to listen for the intonation patterns. Finally, play it a third time, stopping after each one so students can repeat. They can then practise in pairs before talking about the Internet suffixes. Play the recording with the four additional e-mail addresses enough times for students to write them down. Have them read the answers back to you.

Answers

7. lemongrass2272@shotmail.com
8. nsgo7891@shotmail.com
9. www.jazzman/CDs.co.uk
10. dellerh@wmin.ac.uk

Finish up by discussing the questions at the end as a class or in small groups. Extend this by feeding in other connected questions. For example:
Do you ever open attachments?
Do you get a lot of spam/junk e-mail?
Do you like using e-mail?
What are some disadvantages to using e-mail?

5 Speaking

Use these questions to follow on from **4 E-mails and website addresses**. Tell students about something romantic you've done or about a special song. Explain *obsessed with computers* if necessary. Ask for other things people can become obsessed with (movies, cars, another person, oneself). Get students in small groups for this task. You can go around monitoring, collecting examples of language to give feedback on when they've finished.

You could use the photographs of romantic things as a basis for a role play. Have students work in pairs writing a dialogue between a couple. One of them is surprising the other with one of the romantic activities in the pictures.

6 Speaking

Make sure students know what *a chat room* and *a search engine* are. Then have them ask each other for recommendations. Give them some expressions to use:
Do you know any good search engines/sites for jokes?
What's the address?
Is it free?
Just type '…' in a search engine and you'll find it.

Finish up by having students share their suggestions with the whole class.

Using grammar

1 Three classic mistakes

The reading task is used to contextualise the use of the present perfect and the past simple. Lead in by asking students if they have any computer horror stories and then tell them to read about the first classic mistake. When they've finished, ask them to share their reactions in pairs and predict the next two mistakes.

You can either have students read the rest of the text (page 175) in class or at home. Alternatively, just tell them the other mistakes: not backing up your work regularly and opening an attachment without first checking with the person who sent it.

Point out the collocations for *mistake: classic mistake, avoid mistakes, make mistakes.* Encourage students to find other collocations in the text. Also, draw their attention to the word *stuff.* This is another useful word like *thing,* which we often use when we don't know or don't want to say the specific noun. Give students some other examples:
I need some stuff for my hair.
Can I leave some of my stuff in your garage until I find a place to live?
I wonder what that red stuff is on the chicken.

2 Present perfect and past simple

Students are again led towards developing rules based on the examples they have seen. Have pairs of students discuss the four examples. As a class have them suggest a 'rule' and write it on the board. They can then read the explanations and modify their rule if necessary.

When checking the answers to 1–3, ask students to explain their choices. When students underline the examples of the two tenses, point out that the examples of the past simple contain several useful computer expressions.

Answers

1a. *(I did history at university)* sounds more natural. The focus is on a particular time period in the past.
2b. *(Hello, I think we've met before, haven't we?)* sounds more natural. The speaker recognises the other person NOW *(present result)*. This must be because they met at some unspecified point in the past.
3a. *(Oh, you've had a haircut!)* sounds more natural. The focus is on the fact that your hair is shorter – a present result – but the action of having your hair cut obviously occurred at some unspecified time in the past.

The examples of the present perfect in the text are:
In part 1: *I've made them all*
In part 2: *without first checking who has sent it to you* and *if – like me – you've made all these mistakes yourself*

The examples of the past simple are:
In part 1: *the first was to load, I loaded everything, I downloaded lots of free software, My hard drive was full of stuff I never used, This slowed my machine down, I wanted to throw it out the window*
In part 2: *The second classic mistake was not to, I lost a whole morning's work, I got a virus which wiped my hard drive clean*

---

3 Practice

Students can work on this exercise in pairs, alternately saying the sentences and then going back and doing the ones they didn't do before. Write the present perfect expressions on the board:
I've almost finished it.
I've eaten them all already./I've already eaten them.
I've just had …
I've forgotten most of it already.
I've just heard that …

Ask students to think of other examples that are true for them, and where they can respond with these expressions. Draw their attention to the position of the adverbs *(almost, already and just).*

Answers

1. I started reading the new Harry Potter book last week. I've almost finished it.
2. I bought some grapes this morning. I've eaten them already./I've already eaten them.
3. I got my new car yesterday. I've just had an accident.
4. I studied English at school. I've forgotten most of it already./I've already forgotten most of it.
5. I sat my exams in May. I've just heard that I've passed!

4 Linked questions

This exercise shows how we use the present perfect to ask about an experience, and then switch to the past simple when we want to focus on the details. Remind students that *have* is stressed in *Yeah, I have actually.* Model the example with a student and then get the class to do 1–7 in pairs. Point out that if you *didn't get round to something*, you didn't have time to do it, and that if you *get rid of something*, you throw it away or, in the case of a virus, remove it.

Students can then ask each other questions starting with *Have you ever ... ?* Remind them that they can also respond *No, never, but I have* ... . For example:
A: *Have you ever been to a football match?*
B: *No, never, but I have been to a rugby match.*
A: *Did you enjoy it?*
B: *Yeah, it was good.*

Students can do this task in pairs or move around the class, asking each other.

Answers

1. Have you ever been to Rome? Did you see the Sistine Chapel?
2. Have you ever been to Greece? Did you go to Delphi?
3. Have you ever been to America? Did you go to New York?
4. Have you ever been to Asia? Did you go to Thailand?
5. Have you ever loaded on too much software? Did you manage to remove most of it?
6. Have you ever forgotten to save your work? Did you lose all of it?
7. Have you ever got a virus? Did you manage to get rid of it?

5 Time expressions

This is a review of some of the time expressions that students met in Unit 2. This exercise reinforces the difference between those that refer to a specific time in the past (e.g. *last Christmas*) and those that refer to a period that extends from a time (specific or not) in the past to the present (e.g. *for ages*). After checking the students' answers, have them make examples about their best friends, other classmates, or other people.

Answers

Expressions like a: 1, 3, 5, 7 and 8.
Expressions like b: 2, 4, 6, 9 and 10.

6 Always/never

Along with *ever*, these adverbs refer to a general time. Check that students understand the meaning of each example before doing the exercise. *Yet* is sometimes difficult; explain that it refers to an action that has not happened so far up to the present but will probably happen in the future. Point out that *yet* is used this way in questions and negative statements.

When going through the answers, ask students to explain their choices. If they haven't noticed, point out that *any* and *anything* occur with *never*. Also, in many of the sentences with *always*, the verb or adjective is stronger than normal: *love* (instead of *like*), *quite good* (instead of just *good*) and *terrible* (instead of *bad*). Have students talk about any of the sentences that are true for them, and then complete the sentence starters with personalised examples. Encourage students to record these in their notebooks.

Answers

1. never	2. always	3. never	4. always	5. never
6. always	7. never	8. always		

7 How long? When?

This exercise reminds students that *how long* refers to a period of time and can often be used with the present perfect, when that period extends to the present, while *when* refers to a specific time, and when it refers to the past, it is often used with the past simple. The exercise also focuses on those verbs that can refer to actions that happen or states that exist over an extended period of time (e.g. *be, know, work, have*) and those that usually don't happen or exist over extended periods of time (e.g. *meet, get (married), decide, leave, buy*).

Practise the example conversation with students before having pairs ask each other. Remind them that they can respond in any way they like. Extend the exercise by having them ask each other similar questions that are

applicable to their situation. For example:
How long have you had red hair?
When did you leave school/university?

Answers

1. How long have you known your girlfriend? When did you meet her?
2. How long have you been married? When did you get married?
3. How long have you been a vegetarian? When did you decide to stop eating meat?
4. How long have you worked for IBM? When did you leave Compugraphics?
5. How long have you had this job? When did you get it?
6. How long have you had a car? When did you buy it?

8 Further practice

This exercise reinforces the concepts in the previous exercises. You can have students work individually through the exercise before comparing their answers in pairs. As an alternative, read the completed story to the class, while they listen with their Coursebooks closed. Then read it again, but this time include the words in the gaps and don't tell them the verb: *Even though I like England, I BLANK always BLANK to work abroad, ...* Students can then shout out the completed expression (e.g. *I've always wanted to work abroad*). Continue like this for each gap. Students can then complete the exercise in their books.

Answers

1. 've always wanted   2. never thought   3. saw
4. looked   5. filled in   6. sent   7. didn't hear
8. e-mailed   9. spent

Real English

Refer students to the **Real English** note on *a real panic*. Tell them about a time you were in *a real panic* or *a real hurry*. Ask them if they have ever felt this way. What did they do?

Using vocabulary

1 General advice

Go over the four examples. Play the recording of the four examples once all the way through. Then play it again, pausing after each example so that students can repeat. Pay attention to the intonation in each case. Students can then complete the dialogues. Play the recording so students can check their answers, and then

have them practise reading the dialogues in pairs. Write these patterns on the board to reinforce the structures that follow:
Why don't you try + noun/-ing form
Have you tried + noun/-ing form?
You could try + noun/-ing form
If I were you, I'd (just) + verb

Also draw students' attention to some typical responses when people give advice:
Thanks. I hadn't thought of that.
Maybe I'll give them/it a try.
Yeah, you're probably right.

Answers

1. doing a search
2. the petrol station down the road
3. nicotine patches
4. wait and improve your English a bit more, taking it next year
5. pressing Alt, Control, Delete, turn it off and switch it back on again

The sentences giving advice are:
1. Have you tried doing a search?
2. I guess you could try the petrol station down the road.
3. Have you tried nicotine patches?
4. If I were you, I'd wait and improve your English a bit more. You could try taking it next year.
5. Have you tried pressing Alt, Control Delete? I'd just turn it off and switch it back on.

2 Giving computer advice

This exercise gives students the opportunity to use the language from **1 General advice**. Have them work in pairs, alternately asking for and giving advice. Ask if anyone has ever had these problems, what they did and whether it worked. You may want to ask if students have other computer problems and get the class to give them some advice.

3 Keep + -ing

Refer students to **2 Giving computer advice** to find the two examples of this structure, and go over the explanation. You could compare it to the use of *always* with the present continuous from the previous unit. The matching task practises the structure and also reinforces several collocations. Ask students if they can think of other things that can *crash, freeze* and *break down*.
For example:
a screen (pipes, water) can freeze
a computer (the market, the stock market) can crash
a car (a machine, talks) can break down

Answers

1. d.   2. b.   3. c.   4. a.

The second task also includes several collocations. Have students underline those that are new to them and record them in their notebooks. You can follow up by having students change any of the sentences to make them true for them. For example:

My dad keeps saying I should become a doctor.

They can then talk about them with a partner.

4 | Further practice

This exercise provides a chance for recycling the language for giving advice. Encourage students to give each other advice when they talk about the last two questions. Finish up by telling the class of any personal experiences. You could extend this by asking pairs of students to role-play a dialogue between Simon and Pete's (from the conversation on page 64) partners, discussing their annoying habits and offering each other advice. For example:

You know, he's really nice but he keeps on spending all our money on surprise weekend trips.

5 | Speaking

Play the recording of the three stories while students just listen, and then play the recording again while students follow along in their Coursebooks. Then have them decide which story was the most embarrassing. Before having them discuss the questions in the next task in pairs, tell them about any personal experience you have, or alternatively use this one:

I have this friend who was working on some English teaching material for the school website. After she finished, she did a spell check to make sure everything was OK. There were no problems, and she posted the material. A few weeks later, a student asked his teacher what 'gerbils' were. The teacher explained, but the student still looked confused. He wanted to know about the grammatical structure 'gerbils' not the animals. Now the teacher was confused. The student explained that he had read all about them on the website. It turned out that the student had been looking at a section called 'Gerbils and Infinitives'. The spell-checker hadn't liked the word 'gerunds' and had changed them all to 'gerbils'.

6 | Opposites

In this exercise, students can work individually or in pairs. Tell them that the words they are looking for occur in the same order in the text. Remind them to record complete expressions if they want to transfer any to their notebooks.

7 | Advantages and disadvantages

Explain the task and then let students look back through the unit or through their notebooks for useful language. They can then work in pairs, coming up with their lists. Alternatively, divide students into two groups: one thinking of advantages, the other of disadvantages. Then make groups of four, two from each side, to debate the issue. In either case, write some useful language on the board. For example:

They take up too much time.
It's much more convenient.
They've simplified/complicated things.
Remember Y2K?
They're anti-social.

Follow-up

To recycle some of the language from this unit, have students role-play a job interview for a computer support person. As a class, brainstorm a list of requirements (both personal and technical). Then have students work in pairs writing the dialogue between the boss of a small company and the applicant. Write some sentence starters to help get them started:

Have you had much experience with ... ?
Have you ever ... ?
How long have you ... ?
When/why did you leave ... ?
What would you do if ... ?

Students can then practise reading it before performing it to another group.

Unit overview

General topic
Making plans and arranging times and places.

Dialogue
Jamie, Martin and Rachel discuss plans for celebrating Rachel's birthday.

Language input

- Prepositional phrases for location: *at the station, by the main exit, at the bus stop, just in front of the post office,* etc.
- Suggesting alternative times to meet: *Can we make it a bit later?* etc.
- Expressions to show you don't mind: *I'm easy. It's up to you. I'm not bothered.*
- Verbal expressions followed by the *-ing* form or infinitive: *Do you fancy going … ? Would you like to go … ? I'd rather go …*
- Choice questions: *Do you want to do it now or shall we do it tomorrow?*

Language strip

Use the language strip as a way to lead in to the unit. Ask students to look quickly through the list and find any expressions that they have used or could have used before. Explain that in this unit they will learn ways to talk about making plans to meet people. Encourage them to choose some other expressions in the strip that look interesting and to find out more about them.

Use the language strip later on in this unit for a small group task. Ask students to choose four statements and come up with what was said to prompt each one. For example:

A: *Where is he? He should have been here forty minutes ago.*

B: *Ring him on his mobile.*

You could also ask them to find all the expressions that contain a modal auxiliary (e.g. *Shall we meet after work? Can we make it nine? I'll be under the clock*).

You might need to explain some of the following expressions:

- If you say *I'm easy* when someone gives you a choice of things to do, you don't mind which one you do, and are asking the other person to make the choice for you. For example:
  A: *Do you want to sit here or outside?*
  B: *I'm easy. You decide.*

- If you *pick someone up,* you collect them from one place to take them somewhere else – usually in your car. For example: *I'll pick you up around seven, OK?*

- You say *Can we make it … ?* with a time when someone suggests a time to do something and you want to do it at another time. For example:
  A: *How about if I pick you up at eight?*
  B: *Can we make it nine? I don't finish work until eight.*

- A *foyer* is the entrance hall of a hotel, cinema or theatre. In American English, this is called *a lobby.*

- A *mobile* is a mobile phone. For example: *I'll have my mobile with me, so give a ring if there's any problem.*

Remind students to record any of the expressions that they like in their notebooks.

Lead in

You can use **1 Speaking** to lead in to this unit.

Using vocabulary

1 Speaking

First, have students guess how old each person is. They can use the structure *He/She looks about* to begin the activity. Then ask the class to brainstorm all the different people each person might meet. In pairs, they can then discuss where they think each person would usually meet the different people they know. You could finish by asking students to discuss which of the four people they think would have the best social life and why.

2 Waiting for ages!

Use the questions to lead in to the reading task, either in small groups or as a whole class. Explain that if you arrive *just on time,* you get there exactly at the time you planned. Give students some other examples of expressions with *just* connected with meetings. For example:

I was just leaving when you rang.

I just made it.

It might be interesting to divide the class into two groups, male and female, to discuss these questions. When students have finished, have them get into mixed gender groups of three or four to see if men and women answer differently.

Explain the situation of the reading text and have students read it to themselves. They can then share their reactions in pairs. Ask them if they remember what *a rough area* means and to explain why they think the writer described Moss Side as *a rough area* (there is a lot of drug dealing and prostitution there). Play the recording of the text as students follow in their Coursebook. Encourage students to underline any expressions or collocations they are interested in. You may want to point out these expressions connected with meeting people:

sit somewhere by myself
she is always worried about being left on her own in a bar
she finally turned up
I was beginning to worry
sorry, I'm late
So that I didn't have to wait around for you
spoil the evening

Remind students to add the expressions to their notebooks.

3 Speaking

Lead in to this task by telling the class who you are most like, and then tell them a waiting story of your own. Encourage the class to ask you questions and then to recall any expressions that you used. Write these on the board to help students when they tell their own stories in small groups.

4 Prepositional phrases

Prepositions cause learners of English a lot of problems. Remind students that they are best learnt in phrases, as is the case here. Before doing the task, elicit a list of potential meeting places (e.g. *bars, coffee shops, cinemas*) and then ask *Whereabouts exactly in these places can you meet?* Listen to students' suggestions without correcting them. This gives you a chance not only to hear how well they use prepositional phrases, but also where they are lacking in specific vocabulary to describe different parts of a place.

Have students do this exercise in pairs and then compare answers with a partner. After you've clarified any problems, students can test each other in pairs: one person reads the beginnings 1–7 while the other person tries to remember as many of the three possible endings as they can. You should explain that *bit* in f. means *part*.

Tell students to record any prepositional phrases or collocations in their notebooks.

Answers
1. c.   2. g.   3. a.   4. b.   5. d.   6. e.   7. f.

5 Speaking

Use the pictures on page 71 to practise these prepositional phrases. Students can take it in turns describing where people are and then turn it into a memory game. One student closes the Coursebook while the other tries to remember where each person was. For example:
I think the people in the picture on the right were in a pub.

You could also use the pictures to revise the past simple and past continuous tenses in storytelling. Ask students to use sentences starters like:
Last week I was at the airport, when suddenly ...
While I was waiting for my friend in the pub the other day, ...

6 Pronunciation: weak forms

Explain to students that the schwa, /ə/, is common in prepositional phrases because it allows us to say them quickly and smoothly. As you play the recording, ask students to listen for the sound and then play it again, while students listen for the word that has the most stress. Play the recording a third time, pausing after each sentence, so students can repeat.

After students have put the dialogues in order and checked their answers from the recording, point out how *then* is often used at the end of questions as a way of checking or inviting the other person to comment. Have pairs of students practise these dialogues and then tell them to work with a new partner having similar conversations about places in the town/city where they are studying or the area around the school. Go around making sure they are using the weak forms.

Answers
1. c., a., b.
2. c., a., b., d.
3. b., e., f., d., a., c.

7 Speaking

Tell students about the places where you meet people before having them discuss these questions in groups. Write some useful phrases on the board. For example:
It's really convenient.
A lot of young people hang out there.
It's a great spot for ...

Listening

1 Speaking

This task leads in to the listening task. Start off by asking students the questions. Ask if there are any particular traditions that they have now or remember when they were younger. Talk about yourself too. Then get students to individually rank the activities. Point out the collocations *have a quiet meal* and *close friends and family*. Give students some more expressions with *have a quiet …* (*night in, drink, word with someone*). Write some expressions on the board for when they compare rankings:

That's what I'd really like to do.
That's not really my kind of thing.
I used to like doing that, but I'm getting too old for it now.
That's not very exciting, is it?

2 While you listen (Rachel's birthday)

Explain the situation and ask students to listen for what Rachel, Jamie and Martin decide to do and not to do for Rachel's birthday. Play the recording, making sure that students cover the text. Get them to discuss the answers in pairs. Tell them to keep the text covered as they do this.

Answer

They end up deciding to go bowling. They're going to meet at eight in the foyer of the bowling alley near the station. Martin is going to tell Stella and Mike so they can join them. (They decide against going to a musical and Ben's café to hear jazz.)

Next, let students read the conversation as you play the recording again. Then ask students, in pairs, to fill in the first two or three gaps from memory before you play the recording again, this time with pauses so that they can check and fill in the missing words. Do this two or three gaps at a time until the end. Play the recording through one more time with students following the text. If you want students to read the conversation, or parts of it, in pairs, use the tapescript on page 151. The missing words are highlighted in colour.

Answers

Words in gaps in the conversation:

1. They're lovely	9. Can we make it
2. fancy doing	10. give them a ring
3. I'm easy	11. don't you
4. making	12. actually
5. supposed to be	13. middle of the week
6. Ben's	
7. somewhere else	
8. do you fancy going	

You may need to explain a couple of expressions:

- If a place like a café or restaurant *does* something, they offer it. For example: *They do a curry night every Monday. They do a mixture of old soul and R &B on Sundays.*
- If you *chill out*, you relax, often after you have done something tiring. For example: *Thanks for the invitation, but I think I'm just going to go home and chill out.* Refer students to the **Real English** note on *chill out*.

Encourage students to go back through the conversation and add any expressions that they find interesting to their notebooks.

3 Speaking

Students can discuss these questions, which follow on from the conversation, in small groups. Explain that if someone is *fussy*, they aren't easy to please, or they are worried about small details. For example:
We can never decide on the best place to meet after work. Everyone's so fussy. It's either too noisy, too smoky or too expensive.

Also, explain that if you *go along with someone's suggestion*, you agree with it. When students have finished, tell them to close their Coursebooks and ask you the questions.

4 Role play

Before students work on the role play, brainstorm a list of useful expressions for each situation and write them on the board. You might also want to give them the opening lines:

A: *Hello?*
B: *Hi. Martin here. I just wanted to let you know …*

A: *Hello. Moortown Bowling.*
B: *Hello. I was wondering if I could …*

Go around helping with language difficulties and then have students practise a few times together before acting it out to another pair.

5 Time expressions

This exercise focuses on time expressions following *Can we make it … ?* Go over the examples, modelling the pronunciation and then explain the task. You might want to do the first one as an example. Ask students to pay attention to the sentence(s) following the question. Explain that the clue to completing the exercise can be found there. As you go through the answers, ask questions, focusing on some of the other language used. For example:
How long is 'for ages', a relatively short or long time?

What time would you need to leave home to get to school on time?

What are some TV programmes that you don't want to miss?

What places can you be 'away from'? (work, home, my desk)

Why might you need to take a day off work? How about an hour or a year?

> **Answers**
>
> 1. eight   2. later   3. earlier   4. six
> 5. next week some time   6. some other time

Have students go back and underline the examples where the time expression is not specific (*a bit later/earlier, next week some time, some other time*).

6 Free practice

If you want to make the first task a little easier, write a couple of key words on the board to help students remember. For example:
1. work ... seven
2. meeting ... five ... ages
etc.

After pairs of students compare their answers for the second task, ask them to practise the conversations using their different reasons.

7 I'm easy

Go over the examples with the class and practise the pronunciation, particularly the stress pattern in *It's up to you*. When students find these expressions in the dialogue, remind them to look at words around them too. For example:
Whatever. I'm easy. It's up to you, really.

Briefly discuss the questions as a class before having students complete the dialogues.

> **Answers**
>
> 1. easy
> 2. don't
> 3. up
> 4. easy
> 5. bothered
> 6. to

Point out the expression *Whenever suits you*. Practise the pronunciation with the class and then ask a few questions and have students respond with *whenever suits you* or *whatever suits you*. For example:
When shall we have a test?
Do you want to do this exercise now or wait till tomorrow?
Shall I play the recording first or do you want to read it first?

Have pairs of students practise the conversation and then make similar conversations. (Note that if you wanted to be annoying, the conversation could go on for a long time.)

Using grammar

1 The *-ing* form and the infinitive

This area of grammar can cause a lot of frustration for students. There are no practical rules for determining whether a gerund or infinitive is used, and although students probably 'know the rule' that modal auxiliaries are followed by the verb without *to*, they often still make mistakes. As always, remind them that recording these verb phrases in expressions will help.

After going through the explanations, students can test each other in pairs. One person says *Do you fancy ... ?* and the other, without looking at the Coursebook, responds with *going ... ?*

2 Practice

Students can work individually and then check their answers from the recording. Then have them practise the conversations in pairs. Point out and explain, if necessary, some of the other expressions used here:
that new Moroccan place
It might be a laugh.
It might be nice to get out of town.
a friend of mine

Have students go back and underline the complete expressions.

> **Answers**
>
> 1. going, stay   2. going, try   3. To go, to do   4. To go, invite   5. To go, stay   6. go, to go

3 Further practice

Before getting students to do the task, model the first item as an example with a student:
A: *Do you fancy going swimming later?*
B: *To be honest, I'd rather just go for a run.*

Encourage students to use different expressions for making suggestions. Then have them work with another partner for the second part.

Answers

Possible answers:

1. A: Do you fancy going swimming later?
   B: To be honest, I'd rather just go for a run. It's a bit too cold.

2. A: Do you want to go to visit my parents this weekend?
   B: To be honest, I'd rather stay home and catch up with work. I've got an important deadline to meet.

3. A: Would you like to go to a concert next Friday?
   B: Yeah, that'd be great. Shall I phone now and book tickets? They might sell out.

4. A: Do you fancy going to that new club tonight?
   B: I'd rather go to Rock City instead. It's cheaper.

5. A: Do you fancy eating Chinese for dinner tonight?
   B: I'd rather eat Mexican instead. I had some egg rolls for lunch.

6. A: Shall we go to a café for lunch?
   B: Yeah, that'd be great. Do you want to go to that new place round the corner? I hear it's really good.

Refer students to the **Real English** note on *that new club*.

4 The *-ing* form, infinitive with *to* or infinitive without *to*?

This exercise also revises expressions with *get used to*, *make* and *let* from previous units. When you have checked students' answers, they can ask each other in pairs. Alternatively, give each student a number from 1 to 8 and ask them to memorise the corresponding question. They then go around asking their question to other students. Have students record the complete expressions in their notebooks.

Answers

1. using 2. stay 3. learn 4. doing 5. To do 6. doing
7. do 8. going

---

5 Do you want to ... or shall we ... ?

Some students may be curious about the use of *shall*. These days it is common in conversational British English for making offers and suggestions. In American English it is less common. When checking the answers, model the pronunciation, in particular the intonation pattern of choice questions with just two options (rising on the first choice, falling on the second). Then students can practise in pairs.

Answers

1. c. 2. a. 3. e. 4. b. 5. h. 6. d. 7. f. 8. g.

For the second task go over the example, pointing out the use of *just* and ask the tag question *shall we?* that follows sentences starting with *Let's*. Encourage students to follow a similar pattern. When the pairs of students have finished, have a few of them share their answers with the whole class.

6 Free practice

Allow students a few minutes to look back through the unit, including the language strip, and then to think about the details of their plan. To make this easier, you might want to give each student a weekly or monthly calendar so they can note down the dates and times. Go over some expressions for turning down invitations. For example:
I'm afraid I'm busy that day. Could we make it another time?
I'm sorry I won't be able to make it.
I'm ... er ... washing my hair then.

Follow-up

Have pairs of students imagine that they are a company that sets up dates between young people by organising an activity illustrated in one of the pictures on page 75. They should work out the details of how it actually works: what the couple do, the price, etc. Have students then explain their ideas to the rest of the class. You can then get them to vote on the most interesting or unusual ideas. Then ask students to imagine that they have just come back from one of these events and have them write about their experiences.

11 Transport and travel

Unit overview

General topic
Talking about different means of transport and journeys.

Reading
Stereotypes of people who drive certain vehicles.

Language input

- Number adjectives: *a two-hour drive, a fifteen-minute wait*, etc.

- Driving vocabulary: *looks in his mirror, goes through red lights*, etc.

- Comparatives and superlatives: *The sooner, the better. It's much cheaper than it used to be. It's one of the best places to eat in town.*

- Transport collocations: *We got delayed in Rome. It's a very fast line. We broke down just outside Durham. The sea was a bit rough.* etc.

Language strip

Use the language strip as a way to lead in to the unit. Ask students to look quickly through the list and find any expressions that are true about themselves (e.g. *I can't drive*). Explain that in this unit they will learn ways to talk about different kinds of transport and journeys. Encourage them to choose some other expressions in the strip that look interesting and to find out more about them.

Use the language strip later on in this unit for a small group task. Ask students to find those expressions that are connected with planes (e.g. *The flight took eleven hours*), cars (e.g. *I drive a Volvo*), trains (e.g. *We had to stand all the way*) and ships (e.g. *I get seasick just thinking about ferries*). There is another exercise like this later on in the unit. You could also ask students to find those expressions containing a verbal expression followed by an infinitive without *to* (*Shall we get a cab?*) and those followed by an *-ing* form (*I don't mind going by coach, actually*).

You might need to explain some of the following expressions:

- There is a stereotype that someone who drives *a Volvo* is safe, sensible and boring.

- If you *stop over somewhere* on a flight, your plane lands and remains at the airport for a time before continuing on to the final destination. *Dubai* is part of the United Arab Emirates.

- You might say *We had to stand all the way* when talking about a train journey. For example: *By the time I get the train, there are no seats left and I have to stand all the way.*

- If you describe a flight as *a bit bumpy*, you mean there was some turbulence. For example: *Why does it always get bumpy when they bring round the coffee?*

- *An accident black spot* is one part of a road where lots of accidents happen – often, there is a sharp corner there.

Remind students to record any of the expressions that they like in their notebooks.

Lead in

One way to lead in to this unit is to write *car, train, plane* and *coach* on the board and to have groups of students brainstorm the advantages and disadvantages of travelling by each. Elicit some adjectives like *expensive, convenient, fast, comfortable*, etc. so that they can make comparisons. This will give you a chance to assess how well students use comparative and superlative structures, an area covered later on in the unit.

Reading

1 Speaking

Use these questions to lead in to the reading task. Start off by asking students to guess what kind of car you have (or would have if you don't have one). Encourage them to explain their reasoning. For example:
You've got kids, so you've probably got a big car.
You look like the kind of person who drives one of those new minis.

You can then get students in small groups to do the same. If most of your students don't have cars, tell them to discuss what car they think each other would have.

You can then talk about the two patterns. Explain that we often use the expression *tend to* to avoid making too big an overgeneralisation. Give them an example for each pattern:
People who drive red cars tend to speed.
People who drive black cars use them to pretend they are important.

You could extend this activity by asking what characteristics students associate with different colours. This can be quite interesting in multicultural classes.

Have students discuss the pictures of vehicles in pairs. Write some sentence starters on the board. For example:

A driver of a vehicle like this is probably a …
A driver of a vehicle like this probably uses it for …

Before going on to the reading, ask if anyone actually owns one of the cars in the pictures.

2 While you read

Explain that the article students are going to read is a list of stereotypes from Britain. After they have read through the text, they should discuss the answers and their reactions with the same partner they worked with in **1 Speaking**.

> **Answers**
>
> 1. D   2. F   3. E   4. C   5. B   6. A

Play the recording of the text as students follow in their Coursebooks. Encourage them to underline any interesting expressions or collocations. You may want to point out or explain the following:

- If you *swear at someone*, you use bad language to abuse them verbally. For example: *How many of you only swear when you're driving?*
- If someone *cuts in front of you*, they move quickly into the same lane without leaving themselves or you much room to manoeuvre.
- *Hippies* were part of a big youth movement in the late 1960s. They grew their hair long, took lots of drugs and believed in peace and love.
- If you *don't get round to doing something*, you don't do what you were planning to do because you haven't got the time. For example: *I'm sorry I haven't got round to finishing the homework. I've been really busy.*
- If something is *customised*, it has been changed to make it more personal or unusual. We talk about *customised cars* or *customised computers*.

Tell students to record the expressions they find in their notebooks.

3 Speaking

These questions can be discussed in small groups. If possible have all-male and all-female groups. Then after students have finished talking, get the whole class together to compare ideas to see if there are any gender differences.

4 Number adjectives

Students are often confused about this aspect of English. Have them read the two examples from the article. Check that they know what the expressions mean

before asking the question and going over the explanation. Students can work individually on the task and then check their answers in pairs. Make sure they are hyphenating the two parts of the adjective. For extra practice, they can test each other: one person reads the first part while the other reformulates it into a number adjective without looking at the Coursebook.

> **Answers**
>
> 2. It's a three-hundred-pound suit.
> 3. I had a fifteen-minute wait.
> 4. She's got a five-year-old son.
> 5. I did a four-mile jog/run.
> 6. It's a fifteen-minute ride by bus/bus ride.
> 7. It's a two-week cruise.

Students can then talk about the questions in pairs.

5 Driving vocabulary

To lead in to this task, write the word *driver* on the board. Ask students to suggest or use their dictionaries to find adjective collocations. Here are some examples:
a dangerous/reckless/bad/careful/safe/experienced + driver

Ask students to decide which are negative and which positive. You can then have them discuss the questions as a class or in small groups. As you check the answers, ask questions to check they understand the meaning and to extend their knowledge of these expressions. Here are some suggestions:
What should you do if your indicators aren't working, then?

Is it legal to talk on your mobile while you're driving? And to text on it?

Do you think it's true that men just check the map rather than ask for directions?

What do you do when someone cuts in front of you?

Why do you think they're called 'blind corners'? How would you say it in your own language?

> **Answers**
>
> 1. c.   2. d.   3. a.   4. e.   5. b.   6. h.   7. i.   8. f.
> 9. j.   10. g.

Have students discuss the questions in pairs and tell each other about any experiences they have had. Tell the class an example so they can see how the sentence frames work. For example:
I was in the car with my best friend once and we almost had an accident because he overtook this bus on a blind corner. Fortunately, the car coming in the opposite direction swerved out of the way.

This is a good way to review the past tense of irregular verbs.

Using grammar

1 Comparatives and superlatives

This exercise introduces some common expressions containing comparatives and superlatives. Explain the situation and play the recording. Make sure students cover the dialogue. Then have them quickly check their answer in pairs before playing the recording a second time while they complete the gaps. Once they have finished, they can check their answers with you. Play the recording one more time before having students practise the conversation in pairs.

Answers

1. (The sooner,) the better.
2. (It's one of) the best places (to eat in town).
3. (so) the cheaper, (the better)
4. (It's) much better (than it used to be).

You may want to point out the following expressions:

- If you say *you're starving*, you are very hungry. For example: *What's for dinner? I'm starving.*

- Ask students if they remember the expression *a bit short of money.*

- If you *go a really roundabout way*, you go to a place by an indirect route. For example: *No, if you come out of exit 9, you have to go a really roundabout way to get to my place. It's better to use exit 12.*

- If you say to someone *We're/I'm off*, you are saying you're leaving. For example: *I'm off. See you next week.*

Refer students to the **Real English** note on *be off.*

You could also check that students know the guidelines for making the comparative and superlative forms. Write some typical phrases on the board with the adjectives gapped out. Ask students to complete them with the correct form. Here are some examples:

They say flying is the ... way to travel. (safe – safest)

There's always someone much ... off than yourself. (bad – worse)

What's the ... flight to New York at the moment? (cheap – cheapest)

£100? That's much ... than I thought it would be. (expensive – more expensive)

2 Speaking

Use these questions to follow on from **1 Comparatives and superlatives**. You could add more questions to practise some more comparative and superlative forms. For example:

Have you ever ordered the most expensive thing on the menu?

Is it true the more expensive the restaurant, the smaller the portions?

Do you think it's safer on the road these days?

Which is the cleanest/fastest/most comfortable underground system/bus system you've ever been on?

3 Comparing now with the past

This exercise provides students with contextualised examples of comparative structures. Lead in by asking students what changes they have noticed in their towns, countries, society, or the world in, say, the last ten years. Listen to their ideas and then have them complete the sentences. When checking their answers, ask what they think the person is talking about. For example, number 1 could be about a new computer and number 8 about a club. Students can then use this information to ask each other questions in the second task.

Answers

1. last 2. before 3. bigger 4. used 5. much 6. bit
7. Time 8. good 9. remember 10. be

Point out the modifiers *much*, *a bit*, and the *as ... as* structures in numbers 8–10. Then have students go back and underline the complete expressions. For example: *It's better than my last one.*

Students can then test each other in pairs: one person reads the incomplete sentence and the other says the complete phrase without looking at the Coursebook. Have the class do the follow-up task in pairs, deciding what the questions would be. Encourage them to use some of the structures they have learned.

4 Comparative phrases

These are fairly common fixed expressions. As you are checking students' answers, practise the pronunciation of these phrases. You could also ask students if they can think of other situations when they might be used. You could review this later on in the class or the next day, by writing each half on a separate slip of paper, making enough slips for each student (and one for yourself if you have an odd number). Tell students to memorise their half and then go around saying it until they find their matching half.

Answers

1. d.   2. f.   3. e.   4. a.   5. c.   6. b.

Follow up with the personalised sentences. Go around helping when necessary. Before having students talk to their partner, model the two examples with a student. Encourage them to add follow-up comments too. For the last task, you may need to explain that if you *have a lie-in*, you sleep later than usual because you don't have to get up. For example:
I think I'll have a bit of a lie-in tomorrow since it's Sunday.

Before students try 7–12, you might need to explain that *As far as … is/are concerned* means *If we are talking about … and* is a way of giving an opinion about the thing being discussed. You might want to help the class by giving your own example for 7. For example:
As far as computers are concerned, I personally think the smaller, the better.

Tell students that they just need to add nouns to 7–12. They will also need to choose *is* or *are*. *Is* should be used for uncountable nouns like *coffee* or *food*, while *are* will be used for plural nouns like *computers* or *desserts*. As they are writing, check their ideas to ensure they make sense and to check they have chosen *is/are* correctly.

Draw students' attention to the two model conversations at the top of the right-hand column and then encourage them to have similar conversations in pairs, using their own ideas from 7–12. They could then change partners and have similar conversations about the other topics suggested. Alternatively, they could work with a partner and write conversations about these topics.

5 Superlatives

This exercise focuses on a common pattern using superlatives. Go over the examples, explaining that if you *give somewhere/something a miss*, you decide against going there or doing it. You should also explain, if necessary, that *a tourist trap* is a place that attracts a lot of tourists and overcharges them; and that if something is *a rip-off*, you pay more for something than it is worth. As you check the answers, tell students examples of places you know. For the last task, you could have students choose places in the town/city they are studying in or their hometown, if this is different.

Answers

1. biggest   2. best   3. most beautiful
4. most expensive   5. worst   6. oldest   7. nicest
8. most interesting

Finish up by writing the patterns on the board and encouraging students to copy them with a few of their personalised examples in their notebooks.
It's one of the … places to …
It's one of the … (places) in …
It's one of the … bits of …

Using vocabulary

1 Speaking

Lead in to the task by telling students about a journey you have taken. Here is an example:
One of the most uncomfortable journeys I've ever taken was in southern China. It was supposed to be a ten-hour bus ride, but it turned out to be more like twenty-four hours. The bus was really small and was crowded with people and baskets of animals. Luckily, I had a seat, but I couldn't actually move my legs much because there was no room with all the stuff that was piled on the bus …
Have students listen and then ask you questions. Repeat the story and have them listen for expressions and collocations. Write the ones they remember on the board. Before asking them to discuss the questions in small groups, go over the suggested structures. Ask for a few volunteers to tell their stories to the class.

2 How was your journey?

To lead in to the task, divide students into four groups. Ask each group to brainstorm collocations and expressions connected with each form of transport in the pictures on pages 80 and 81. You could have students write on big sheets of paper, put them up round the classroom and have students wander around looking at the other groups' work. Then do the exercise, asking students to see if any of their phrases turn up. When students compare their answers, tell them to underline the expressions that helped them.

Answers

2. train   3. car   4. car   5. train   6. plane   7. ferry
8. ferry   9. plane   10. ferry   11. car   12. train

3 Trip expressions

This exercise helps reinforce the expressions from **2 How was your journey?** Once students have completed as many gaps as they can remember and looked back to check, have them test each other in pairs. Then explain that repeating the task from **1 Speaking** will help their fluency and overall performance. Retell your story with some of these expressions too.

Answers

1. a. over	b. did	c. caught	d. got
2. a. just	b. crowded	c. line	
3. a. Traffic	b. down	c. got	d. any
4. a. got	b. sea	c. calm	

4 Listening

Explain the situation and what you want students to do and play the recording. Then get them in groups to discuss their initial reaction. Next, play the recording again so that they can add to their notes. Play the recording one more time as students follow the tapescript on page 152, underlining any expressions they find interesting. You may need to explain that Coventry is a city in the Midlands area of England, and that if you say *something is a pain* or *a pain in the neck*, you mean that it is annoying.

Answers

Speaker 1 travelled by train. He had to stand all the way and the carriage was full of football fans who were drinking and smoking and shouting.

Speaker 2 travelled by plane. Their flight was delayed for two hours and was quite bumpy. Then their baggage was lost and they won't get it back for a couple of days. Finally, they were overcharged for the taxi fare from Gatwick.

Speaker 2 had the worst journey.

5 Speaking

Use the pictures on page 81 to lead in to this task to help generate some ideas. Ask if students have ever had a puncture on their bike, miles from home without a repair kit, or been in a car accident. Explain that in the UK, the Automobile Association (AA) provides road assistance to members if they break down. Ask students what, if any, the equivalent organisations are in their own countries and whether anyone has had to call them out. Give students time to look back at the previous exercises before they come up with their story. You might want to have students write their story for homework.

6 Learner advice: dictionaries

This exercise explicitly reminds students of the importance of collocation and the importance of learning more with words you've met before and the importance of learning to do more with words you've met before. One way to exploit this is to write the seven headwords on the board, pointing out that *stop* here is a noun, and have students in pairs write sentences using them. Then do the exercise. Students can then go back and modify any of their sentences where they have found a more appropriate collocation. Encourage them to record the collocations that are new to them and that seem useful in their notebooks.

Answers

1. cab 2. car 3. stop 4. train 5. bus 6. coach
7. flight

7 Speaking

This exercise follows on from **6 Learner advice: dictionaries,** and is a good opportunity to talk about collocation dictionaries. If you have some available, bring them in to show students and let them compare these with their own dictionaries. If you have access to the Internet, you could also do this with several of the online dictionaries.

If possible, have a collocation dictionary in the class with you and when someone asks you for a good collocation, or when you are giving feedback on collocation errors, give the dictionary to a student to look up suggestions.

Follow-up

Ask pairs of students to choose one of the forms of transport in the pictures on pages 80 and 81. Then explain that they are an advertising team that has been asked to run a promotional campaign to encourage more people to take their chosen form of transportation. They should come up with a slogan and a write a two-minute radio commercial. Tell them that they can talk about the bad things associated with other forms of transportation (e.g. *Tired of bumpy flights, lost luggage and long delays?*). Encourage students to use expressions from the unit. Then divide the class into two big groups with one person from each pair. Each person then performs their commercial.

12 Food

Unit overview

General topic
Talking about different kinds of food and food problems.

Reading
The problem of obesity in developed countries.

Language input

- Vocabulary to describe food: *It's a kind of salad. It's very filling. It's got quite a strange texture.* etc.
- Vocabulary for food-related problems: *They're obese. They've got food poisoning. I can't eat anything with meat in it.* etc.
- Food collocations: *put on weight, a balanced diet, a lovely meal,* etc.
- Expressions with *should've: You should've come. You should've told me before. I shouldn't have asked.* etc.
- Pronunciation of contracted forms: *should've, shouldn't have*

Language strip

Use the language strip as a way to lead in to the unit. Ask students to look quickly through the list and find any expressions that are true for them (e.g. *I'm allergic to nuts*). Explain that in this unit they will learn ways to talk about food and diet. Encourage them to choose some other expressions in the strip that look interesting and to find out more about them.

Use the language strip later on in this unit for a small group task. Ask students to choose several of the expressions that contain *it* or *this* (e.g. *It's very good for you, but I can't stand it myself*) and discuss what is being referred to. Alternatively, ask them to find all the expressions with contractions and to practise saying them.

You might need to explain some of the following expressions:

- *Haggis* is a traditional Scottish food consisting of a sheep's stomach stuffed with minced meat.
- If *you are allergic to something*, you become ill, get a rash or start sneezing when you eat, touch or smell something. For example: *I find a lot more people are allergic to cats and dogs these days.*
- If something is *bland*, it has very little flavour or taste. For example: *This tastes a bit bland. Can you pass the soy sauce?*
- If you say *the house red/white*, you are referring to wine, usually the cheapest one the restaurant offers.

- If food *is* or *has gone off*, it is no longer fresh, and smells or tastes bad. For example: *I think this milk's gone off.*
- If you say *I'm so hungry, I could eat a horse*, you are emphasising that you are very hungry. For example: *What time's dinner? I'm so hungry, I could eat a horse.*
- In England, *Yorkshire pudding* often accompanies roast beef. It is made of flour and water and is savoury, not sweet. Despite its name, it isn't a dessert.
- If you describe food as *yummy*, you are saying it is delicious. You can also say *yum*. For example:
  A: *What's for dinner?*
  B: *Curry. Yum!*
- If you *have a sweet tooth*, you really like eating sweet food.
- If food is *very moreish*, it's so nice, you want more and more of it.

Remind students to record any of the expressions that they like in their notebooks.

Lead in

Ask students to tell you about the most disgusting thing they've ever eaten, what it was, what it tasted like, where they ate it. Then ask them about the most delicious thing. Then show them the pictures of different foods on page 82 and do **1 Different food**.

Using vocabulary

1 Different food

Go over the suggested expressions and practise the pronunciation before having students guess what each food is in pairs. Then ask a few students to share a couple of their ideas. Play the recording so that they can then check their answers. The same pairs can then talk about the food again, now that they know what it is. For example:
It doesn't look very good, but it probably tastes delicious.

Answers
1. E 2. H 3. G 4. F 5. D 6. I 7. A 8. B 9. C

2 Describing food

This exercise focuses on some typical ways of describing food. Point out the modifiers *quite* and *very*. Remind students that when *quite* is stressed, it means *not very* but when the adjective following it is stressed, it means *very*. Also point out the expression *it's a kind of*. When students have checked their answers by listening to the recording again, have them discuss the questions at the end in pairs. At this point you might want to go over the typical structures following sensory verbs. For example:
It looks/tastes/smells good/delicious/awful, etc.

It looks/tastes/smells like a kind of soup/chicken/old socks.

Have students use these different structures to describe some of the pictures.

Answers

Possible answers

1. A   2. D   3. F   4. G   5. I   6. E   7. C   8. H
9. B

---

3 Speaking

This exercise provides more practice using some of the language in the previous exercises. Instead of having students just tell a partner about five different foods, have students walk around describing one food to one person before moving on to speak to another. At the end, ask students to tell you what they learned using these sentence starters:
The food I'd most like to try is …
The food that sounded the most unusual was …
The food that I didn't like the sound of was …

4 English food!

Discuss the questions as a class and then talk about which national and regional cuisines you like. You could also talk about students' perceptions of food from different countries. Ask, for example:
What do you think of as typical American food?
What would you expect to eat if you were staying with a Russian family?

You can then talk about what they think of English food, which doesn't have a very good reputation.

Have students complete the three texts individually and then compare their answers with a partner. Encourage them to record the collocations and complete expressions in their notebooks. Point out the following patterns and ask students to make sentences that are true for them:
I find … a bit/much too …
They're/It's nice and + positive adjective (filling, spicy)

You may need to explain that if you say *you can't beat something*, you think that it is the best thing. For example:
You can't beat a nice cold beer on a hot summer's day.

A *full English breakfast* consists of fried egg, bacon, sausage, grilled tomatoes, fried bread and toast and marmalade.

Answers

1. a. bland   b. comfort   c. prefer   d. sauces
2. a. healthy   b. filling   c. kind   d. limited
3. a. greasy   b. fattening   c. foreign   d. spicy   e. rich

---

Take this opportunity to ask other questions to help extend students' knowledge of these collocations. For example:
What are some examples of comfort food in your country?
What do you think makes a soup filling?
Do you like rich foods?
What are some cafés or restaurants where you find the choice of food a bit limited?

Using vocabulary

1 Before you read

The first part of this exercise introduces some vocabulary for food-related problems as a lead-in to **2 Eat your greens!** For the discussion stage, you might want to review some of the expressions comparing the past with the present if students want to talk about how things are changing:
It's more of a problem now than it was before.
It's not as common as it used to be.

Answers

1. e.   2. a.   3. c.   4. b.   5. d.

---

2 Eat your greens!

Ask students what they think the title is referring to (vegetables). Then ask them to guess which of the problems in **1 Before you read** will be discussed. Have them read the article without worrying about understanding everything and then compare their answers to the three questions with a partner.

Answers

1. The problem is obesity.

2. One suggested cause is that people now tend to have less time to spend on planning and cooking meals, and buying fresh vegetables. They also feel guilty about not spending time with their kids and so give in when their children ask for sweets and chocolates. Another suggested cause is that big food companies spend millions encouraging kids to eat fattening foods.

3. One company has taken flavourings from foods children like – chocolate, baked beans, pizza – and added them to vegetables. They hope this will encourage kids to eat more vegetables.

When students have finished, play the recording again as they follow in the Coursebook. Encourage them to underline expressions and collocations they find interesting and then ask about any they are not sure about. Remind them to add some of these to their notebooks.

3 | Speaking

Use these questions, which follow on from the reading task, in small groups. Explain that if *something catches on*, it becomes popular. Ask students to tell you if they think some other things will ever catch on in a big way, for example, electric cars, portable DVD players or whatever the latest new thing is. When students have finished, ask if they think their answers would be different if they were older, had/didn't have a family or were richer/poorer.

4 | Vocabulary focus

This exercise reinforces some food-related collocations, and adds a few more. Have students work individually or in pairs. When checking their answers, ask them a few related questions. For example:

What kinds of food make you gain weight?

What would you say makes up a balanced diet?

What would a poor diet not include?

Does anyone actually like having a heavy meal at breakfast?

What cuts of meat are generally lean? What are some meats that tend to be fatty?

Tell students a couple of things about yourself so they can see how these collocations can be used:

I'm actually trying to put on a bit of weight because I've just come out of hospital.

I think a nice glass of brandy is good for the digestion.

Then get students to talk about their own ideas in pairs.

Answers

1. weight   2. diet   3. food   4. meal   5. fruit   6. meat
7. salad   8. good

At a later stage in the unit you can revise this by getting one student to come to the front of the class and sit down facing the rest of the students. Write one of the words on the board so that the student at the front cannot see the word, but everyone else can. The class then have to remember different collocations for the word and shout them out – but not the actual word itself – until the student guesses what the word is. The student then goes back and another comes up and the process is repeated with another word.

5 | It should be banned!

Make sure students understand what each of these things in the box are and that some are light-hearted (karaoke, golf and grammar) rather than serious political issues. (You might want to get students to think about why some people might not like these things.) You could also turn this into a debate. Have students pick one of these questions, or come up with one of their own.

Divide students into two groups: one for banning, the other against. Give them ten minutes to think about arguments in support of their respective positions before getting them into groups of four – two from each side – to debate the issue.

6 | I can't eat that!

We often say *I can't eat …* or *I don't eat …* . You might want to explain that *I don't eat …* typically means you've made a conscious decision not to eat it, for example for religious reasons, whereas *I can't eat …* often implies some reason like an allergy. Have students work individually on this task and then compare their answers in pairs. They can also talk about if any are true for them.

Answers

1. f.   .2. a.   3. g.   4. h.   5. b.   6. c.   7. e.   8. d.

You may need to explain that if you *can't stand something*, you really dislike it and that if you *can't be bothered to do something*, you don't want to make the effort to do it. Ask students to tell you what they can't stand or can't be bothered doing. For example:
I can't stand all this rain!

Most days, I can't be bothered to make breakfast in the morning.

7 | Who's the fussiest eater?

Ask if students remember the conversation in Unit 10 when Rachel, Martin and Jamie were talking about where to go and Jamie was being a bit fussy. Then ask them to tell you what they think *a fussy eater* is. Have students spend a few minutes looking through the menu and asking about any of the items they are unsure of. You might need to explain the following:

- *Wasabi* is a kind of hot green mustard usually served with raw fish. It's Japanese.
- *Paté* is a paste.
- *Anchovies* are small fish that are often salted and added to food.
- *Satay* is a dish in which the meat or vegetables are marinated and then barbecued.
- A *lychee* is a kind of reddish fruit with a sweet white inside. It's Chinese.

Have students talk about the menu in pairs.

Using grammar

1 | Listening

Lead in by pointing out the picture on page 86 and asking students to think about if it reminds them of anything. They should then share their thoughts with a partner. You might want to tell the class a story here. For example:
A friend of mine was out on a first date with a very sophisticated woman. He really wanted to impress her, and so he took her to a really fancy restaurant. He pretended to know all about wine, even though he never drinks it, and ordered a bottle of their finest red. Anyway, everything was going well until he reached for the salt and accidentally knocked over the bottle, spilling it all over the woman's white silk shirt.

Have students then ask you questions. For example:
So, did he ever see her again?
Oh, yes, they're a happily married couple now!

Explain the situation in the listening text and go over the three questions. Play the recording and then have students share their answers and reactions in pairs.

Answers

1. No, but they pretended that they did.
2. Steve didn't like most of the food, but said that he did to be polite. Also, the bill was wrong at first and they had to correct it. Then they realised that they didn't have enough cash on them.
3. He might have gone home. He might have had trouble finding the cash machine.
4. Answers will vary.

---

2 | Should've

In order to help students understand the meaning of *should've*, ask them to explain why Cathy used the two examples. Then go over the explanation in the Coursebook and the two other examples. Check that students can see what the present result is (*I'm really hungry. I've got a terrible headache*).

3 | Practice

Students can work through this exercise individually. Check their answers and then have students practise the dialogues in pairs. Next, have one person read the prompt and the other respond from memory. Encourage students to record the responses as whole sentences. You might also want to point out that *could've* in numbers 4 and 5 expresses something that was possible, but that wasn't done.

Answers

1. Well, you should've eaten more at dinner.
2. You should've gone before we came out.
3. Well, you should've brought a coat.
4. You should've told me before! I could've cooked something else.
5. Really! You should've said. We could've done something special.
6. You should've come to the party. It was great fun.

The second task gives more practice with *should've* as well as focusing on some more food collocations. Have students go back and underline the complete expressions.

Answers

1. (I) should've added (some wine or something.)
2. (I told you we) should've brought (an umbrella.)
3. (I knew I) shouldn't have had (all that cream with the cake.)
4. (You) should've come.
5. (You) should've seen (it.)
6. (I knew I) should've gone (to the bank before I came out.)
7. (I) should've ordered (something lighter.)

---

4 | Pronunciation: contractions

Play the recording a couple of times so students get used to the way the contracted forms sound. Then play the recording again, pausing after each sentence so that students can repeat. They can then practise saying them to their partner. For each one, have them read the phrase silently, look up and then say it. This helps them make the contraction because they have to get to the end quickly before they forget.

Get students to discuss the second task in pairs. Choose a few students to share some of their suggestions with the whole class.

Answers

Possible answers:
2. … because now we have to pay this huge bill.
3. … because now I don't have the time to write my thesis.
4. … because now he's on the waiting list.
5. … because now he thinks I'm being nosy.
6. … because now you're in a lot of trouble.
7. … because now I don't have the time to help you.
8. … because now they've decided to paint the whole house a different colour.
9. … because it was good. You feel bad now because you missed it.
10. … because now I feel sick

---

5 | Further practice

Have students read the letter and then talk about it in pairs. Alternatively, have them listen to you read the letter a couple of times before they discuss it. Write some of their suggestions on the board. You might also want to talk about how we can use *never* for emphasis. For example:
They never should've taken the car in the first place!

Here are some suggested answers:
They should've left earlier.
Janet shouldn't have rung her mother.
They really should've booked some seats.
They should've waited and caught the next train.
Janet should never have listened to Nick.
They should've asked someone for directions.
Janet should've kept to the speed limit.
Janet never should've tried to bribe the policeman.

Follow up by dividing the class into pairs. Ask one person to re-read the letter and write all the expressions with *get* (*got to the station, got to the motorway, got a bit lost, get to the wedding, get out of prison*) on a piece of paper, and their partner to do the same with *go* (*five minutes before we were supposed to go, go back home, we went off the motorway, I was sure I was going in the right direction, we went the wrong way again*). Have students close their Coursebooks and use these expressions to help retell the story.

Follow-up

Use the menu on page 85 to develop a role play. Have students work in pairs. One person is a fussy eater and the other can't make a decision (or one person wants the cheapest thing on the menu, while the other person wants a lot). If you get students in groups of three, one person can be the waiter. Brainstorm a list of restaurant language first:
I'll have the …
Are you ready to order?
I need a few more minutes.
What's it got in it?
Does it come with chips?

Have students look through the language strips at the start of this unit and Unit 7 for other useful expressions. Then have them write the dialogue and practise it before acting out their skit to another group or to the whole class.

Review: Units 9–12

The exercises here can be used as a test. However, **4 Look back and check** and **8 What can you remember?** are better done as a discussion in pairs.

1 Grammar review

Answers
1. did you start
2. was, I've ever been to
3. I'd
4. never come
5. You should've been
6. we came
7. keeps cutting out
8. have you had
9. I've forgotten
10. go, stay in

2 Comparing things

Answers
1. nicest
2. coldest
3. most annoying
4. most painful
5. most well-paid
6. most depressing
7. most badly-paid
8. scariest

3 Verb forms

Answers
1. staying
2. to go
3. asking
4. to get
5. getting
6. taking out
7. breaking down
8. to buy
9. walking
10. living

4 Look back and check

Answers will vary.

5 Verb collocations

Answers
1. j.   2. h.   3. i.   4. g.   5. b.   6. c.   7. e.   8. d.
9. f.   10. a.

6 Adjectives

Answers
1. quiet
2. obsessed
3. bland
4. user-friendly
5. wrong
6. awful
7. amazing
8. greasy
9. spicy
10. hopeless

7 Questions and answers

Answers
1. h.   2. f.   3. j.   4. a.   5. d.   6. c.   7. b.   8. e.
9. g.   10. i.

8 What can you remember?

Answers will vary.

9 Common expressions

Answers
1. banned
2. thought
3. have
4. hardly
5. better
6. late
7. going
8. to go
9. bothered
10. mind

Answers for 11–13 will vary.

10 Revision quiz

Answers

1. Possible answers: a hotel, a cinema.
2. Can (Jane) come along?/Can I invite (George)?
3. You use it to move the arrow (cursor) on your computer.
4. *An amateur* is someone who does an activity for the love of it, not as a living. *A professional* is someone who does something as a living. Usually, we talk about amateur/professional sports players, actors, singers, photographers, painters, etc.
5. *Comfort food* is food that makes you feel warm and cosy. Examples include chicken pot pie, macaroni and cheese, etc. Comfort food is good to eat when you're feeling depressed or a bit ill.
6. Possible answers: someone who annoys you, someone you have had a fight with.
7. You're *obese* if you're severely overweight. If you are obsessed with dieting and are seriously underweight as a result, you are *anorexic*.
8. Possible answers: ... asking me out, ... making noises when he eats.
9. Possible answers: at nine, near the ticket counter, on the corner.
10. Possible answers: fruit salad, potato salad, egg salad.
11. Possible answers: it doesn't work, the person (staff) isn't doing the job properly.
12. *Junk food* includes all foods that are bad for your health. *Fast food* is food (usually *junk food*) that you can get quickly at a restaurant or take-away stand. *Junk food* is a negative expression, *fast food* is neutral.
13. It can make your computer crash or wipe your hard drive.
14. If your doctor tells you to, or if you can't eat certain foods.
15. You might stop over at a place if your connecting flight is delayed, or if you'd like to spend some time in that place before flying on to your ultimate destination. Also, with lots of long-distance flights, you can stop over in a city and change planes.
16. You've eaten too much and are uncomfortably full.
17. I don't mind. I'm easy.
18. Ripe fruit.
19. Possible answers: fried food can be too greasy, for example chips; curry can be too spicy; soup, vegetables can be a bit bland if they lack flavour; desserts or food made with a lot of butter, alcohol or cream can be very rich.
20. Possible answers: it hasn't arrived yet, bad weather is holding it up somewhere, it is being inspected.

Unit overview

General topic
Talking about places to see on holiday and the weather.

Dialogue
Two couples on holiday discuss their plans for the day.

Language input

- Vocabulary for different tourist attractions: *a monument, a cathedral, a theme park,* etc.
- *Recommending: I was thinking of trying some local food. Can you recommend anywhere?* etc.
- Holiday collocations: *We went on a guided tour. I must remember to write a few postcards.* etc.
- Describing places: *It's a bit of a rip-off. It's a bit of a tourist trap. You get a great view of the city from up there.* etc.
- Weather vocabulary: *It rained the whole time. The heat was unbearable. It was a bit chilly.* etc.
- Expressions with *going to, will, probably* and *might: I'm just going to have an early night. I don't know, I'll probably just stay in. I suppose I might go travelling.*
- Expressions with *it depends: It depends on the weather. It depends how I feel.* etc.
- Pronunciation: linking final consonants with a following vowel.

Language strip

Use the language strip as a way to lead in to the unit. Ask students to quickly look through the list and find any expressions that they could have said about something they have done in the past (e.g. *What a view! The weather was perfect for sightseeing*). Explain that in this unit they will learn more ways of talking about places to visit and their plans for the day while on holiday. Encourage them to choose some other expressions in the strip that look interesting and to find out more about them.

Use the language strip later on in this unit for a small group task. Ask students to discuss what place they think is being referred to in some of the expressions. For example, *The markets were really great* could be referring to Bangkok. Alternatively, they can think about how to respond to some of the questions (e.g. *What did you think of the National Gallery?*). If it is a yes/no question (e.g. *Did you go to the bazaar?*), they should include a follow-up comment (e.g. *No, we didn't get round to it*).

You might need to explain some of the following places and expressions:

- If something is *well worth a visit*, it is a really good place to go and see. For example: *If you're ever in London, try to go to the Museum of Mankind; It's well worth a visit.*
- *The National Gallery* is a large art gallery in London.
- A *bazaar* is a big market, especially in the Middle East. There are famous bazaars in cities like Cairo and Istanbul.
- A *mummy* is a dead body, usually from long ago, that has been preserved.
- If you *shop till you drop*, you spend a lot of time and energy shopping. For example: *I'm going to spend the weekend in Singapore and I'm planning to shop till I drop.*
- If something is *a total rip-off*, it is not worth the money you pay for it, or you are being overcharged for it. For example: *Don't take the open-air tour bus; it's a total rip-off.*
- The *Impressionists* is a term applied to a group of artists, for example Monet and Renoir, from the late nineteenth century, who painted in a characteristic style.
- The *Acropolis* refers to the ancient Greek citadel overlooking Athens.
- If some friends are *putting you up*, you are staying with them in their house.

Remind students to record any of the expressions that they like in their notebooks.

Lead in

Lead in by asking some general questions about sightseeing. For example:

Do you like to spend time sightseeing, or do you prefer to go to the beach or stay in the bar?

What kind of places do you like to see, historic buildings, museums, old parts of towns, markets?

Do you usually organise your time or just take things as they come?

Do you try to see a little bit of everything or a lot of a few things?

Using vocabulary

1 Sightseeing words

This exercise focuses on several words that are similar in meaning. By using their dictionaries, referring to the pictures, and thinking of examples, students will probably be able to see the differences. When they think of famous examples, you can have them work in pairs initially and then compare their answers with another pair. Then in this larger group, they can make their recommendations.

While going through the answers to the first task, give a few collocations for each place. For example:

a life-size statue of …
a famous monument to …
visit an art gallery
look round the local museum
a local church
a magnificent cathedral
attend prayers in the mosque
a sacred temple
a royal palace
a ruined castle
spend the day at a theme park
there's a funfair in town
an Internet café
a fancy restaurant

Answers

1. A *statue* is of a person, while *a monument* can be anything to remind people of an event or a person.
2. A *gallery* contains works of art, while *a museum* can contain many different objects and artefacts, not necessarily works of art.
3. A *cathedral* is larger and more important than *a church*. Traditionally, a *cathedral* is the seat of a bishop. There are usually one or two cathedrals in a city, but there are many churches.
4. A *mosque* is a place of worship for Muslims, while *a temple* is for Hindus, Buddhists or *Sikhs*.
5. A *palace* is a home for royalty or heads of state, while *a castle* is a large fortified building built long ago.
6. A *theme park* is usually larger than *a funfair* and has a particular theme, while *a funfair* is smaller and often moves from town to town.
7. A *restaurant* tends to have a bigger selection of food and is open for lunch and dinner, while *a café* serves quick snacks and can be open all day.

   a. a cathedral or church
   b. a monument
   c. a restaurant
   d. a theme park

2 Recommending

Students sometimes have difficulty with the verb *recommend*. As well as the phrase *Can you recommend anywhere?* you may want to also give them other phrases as well. For example:
I strongly recommend it.
I wouldn't recommend it.
Can you recommend a good doctor?

Encourage students to record these in their notebooks. Also point out the pattern *I was thinking of* to introduce a tentative plan.

Have students work individually through the task and then play the recording so they can check their answers. After they ask each other to recommend places, ask them to close their Coursebooks and ask you the questions to see if you have the same ideas.

Answers

1. f.　2. e.　3. c.　4. g.　5. a.　6. h.　7. b.　8. d.

Here is information about some of the places mentioned in the responses:
The British Museum in London has a huge collection of historic artefacts from all over the world.
The National Portrait Gallery is next to the National Gallery in London and specialises in portraits.
Parc Asterix is a theme park whose theme is the French cartoon character Asterix (and his friends Obelix, etc.).
Jalan Surabaya is a famous market in Jakarta (the capital of Indonesia).
Broadway refers to the theatre district in New York.
Shinjuku Park is in Tokyo.

3 Collocations

Lead in by asking students to tell you what general things people do on holiday. Students might suggest things like *exchange money* and *take a tour*. Write their suggestions on the board. Then have them do the exercise. After you have checked students' answers, ask if they want to modify any of their previous suggestions, for example, *go on a guided tour, change money at the bank*. Extend the exercise by asking questions. For example:
What things do you like taking photos of?

Do you like having your picture taken?

Can you remember what else, apart from tickets, you can 'book'? (a room, a seat)

What else, apart from a restaurant, can be 'fully booked'? (a flight, a hotel)

You may need to explain that if you *buy something on the black market*, you are not buying it through the proper channels, and so it is illegal.

Answers

1. g.　2. e.　3. i.　4. a.　5. j.　6. b.　7. c.　8. d.
9. f.　10. h.

4 Speaking

Introduce this exercise by telling students about an experience yourself. Again, encourage questions and have them recall any useful phrases that you used. You might want to also feed in other questions practising some of the collocations from **3 Collocations**:

Do you prefer going on guided tours or going round by yourself?

Do you send postcards when you're on holiday?

What do you recommend doing to keep your things safe?

Do you take travellers' cheques or do you use a credit/debit card?

5 What's it like?

Before doing this task, focus students' attention on the pictures and ask them in pairs to describe what kind of place each one is. Write the following patterns on the board to help:

It looks like a …
I think that's in …
That looks like a (adjective) kind of place.
Isn't that the …?

Students can then decide if the descriptions are negative or positive by choosing whether a. or b. follows each one. Check that students understand the expressions by asking questions. For example:

How much should they charge, then?

Why do you think it's a rough area?

Do you think you'd pick up a bargain or get ripped off in a tourist trap?

Then play the recording so students can check their answers. Play the recording again, while students follow the tapescript on page 153. Point out the expressions *thanks for letting me know* and *thanks for telling me*.

Answers

Sentences that can be followed by a: 2, 6, 7 and 8
Sentences that can be followed by b: 1, 3, 4 and 5

Real English

Refer students to the **Real English** note on *a tourist trap*. Tell them about some tourist traps you've encountered in your travels. Ask if they've ever been to a tourist trap. Do they know of any tourist traps near them?

Practise the two examples in the final part of the exercise with two students in front of the class. You could have students walk around having one conversation with one person before moving on to talk about another place with another person.

Listening

1 Speaking

These questions lead in to the conversation. You could use them for a whole class discussion. If so, brainstorm a list of places to stay in: hotels, youth hostels, bed and breakfasts, campsites, caravans, etc. Also, ask further questions. For example:

Did you stay in touch?

Have you ever had a holiday romance?

If you are abroad, do you tend to make friends with people from the same country as you?

You can then get students in pairs to talk about the places in the pictures. The pictures show Paris, New York, Thailand and Buenos Aires. Write some sentence starters on the board:

I'd definitely visit …
I'd probably do a bit of …
Maybe I'd go …

2 While you listen (A day out)

Explain the situation. Then go over the two questions and ask students to listen for the answers. Play the recording, making sure that they cover the text. Get them to discuss the answers in pairs. Tell them to keep the text covered as they do this.

Answers

1. They are visiting Paris. (the Louvre, the Eiffel Tower, Champs Elysée)
2. David and Victoria are more organised.

Next, let students read the conversation as you play the recording again. Then ask students, in pairs, to fill in the first two or three gaps from memory before you play the recording again, this time with pauses so that they can check and fill in the missing words. Do this two or three gaps at a time until the end. Play the recording through one more time with students following the text. If you want students to read the conversation, or parts of it, in pairs, use the tapescript on page 154. The missing words are highlighted in colour.

You may want to point out or explain a couple of expressions:

- If someone asks if it is OK if they do something, you can say *Go ahead* to mean that it is OK. For example:
  A: *Can I borrow your dictionary?*
  B: *Yeah, go ahead.*

- You say *That's a shame* to sympathise with someone about a situation or to expresses that you are sorry about something. For example:

  A: *I'm afraid the restaurant's fully booked.*

  B: *Oh, that's a shame. I was really looking forward to going there.*

- If you *wander around somewhere*, you take your time walking around a place without any definite purpose. For example: *Do you fancy wandering round the cathedral for an hour before we get something to eat?*

Answers

Words in gaps in the conversation:

1. join you
2. comfortable
3. a great view
4. thought about it
5. have a wander round
6. depends
7. gets
8. plans
9. don't really like
10. sounds like
11. clear up
12. what time
13. booked a table
14. probably will
15. afford it

Have pairs of students react to the dialogue by discussing the questions at the end. Ask a few students to tell you what they thought and add a few more adjectives if necessary. For example:

He/she sounds a bit fussy/boring/posh/arty/indecisive.

He/she sounds really easy-going/fun/friendly.

As an extension have groups of four students – or three – if you explain that Jason stayed back at the hotel – role-play the scene at the restaurant where the people talk about how their day was. This is a good chance to review some of the language from the previous units.

3 Talking about the weather

Lead in by asking students what they think the weather is going to be like today, and then if appropriate, what they want it to be like. Refer back to the photographs of places on page 94, and ask what they think the weather's like there. This gives you a chance to react to some of their suggestions and feed in other collocations. For example:

It looks quite cold and misty there.

I bet it gets very humid there.

It looks lovely and clear.

Get students to work through the exercise and then have them compare answers in pairs with one person asking *What's the weather like?* and the other person

responding. Tell them to swap roles halfway through. Before moving on to the next task, tell students to go back and find those collocations and expressions that are new to them and to transfer them to their notebooks. Point out the following time expressions: *the whole time, most of the time, a couple of times, the rest of the time.*

Answers

1. Terrible!   2. Great!   3. Terrible!   4. OK.   5. OK.
6. Terrible!   7. OK.   8. OK.   9. OK.   10. Terrible!

The questions in the second task work best in multinational classes. If your students are all from the same country, ask them to talk about another country they know, or bring in some information, maybe off the Internet, about different places around the world. Give each person in a small group different information to look through quickly. Students can then answer the questions about these places.

4 Weather forecasts

Introduce this exercise by writing these expressions on the board:

We were really lucky with the weather. It …

We didn't have much luck with the weather. It …

Have students use these patterns to talk about the holiday from **3 Talking about the weather**. Then explain that in English we often talk about *luck* or *chance* (e.g. *There's a chance of snow. With luck, it won't rain for you*) with the weather. Ask students why they think that is the case, and then have them do the exercise.

Answers

1. d.   2. b.   3. f.   4. a.   5. e.   6. c.

Have students practise the expressions *but with any luck* and *knowing our luck*, and then have them practise saying the sentences in pairs with one person asking *Have you heard the forecast?* and the other person responding.

Using grammar

1 Going to, will probably, might

Students may have learnt that *will* is used to talk about the future in English. However, just like the weather, the future can be predicted with varying degrees of certainty, and so we use different forms to express it.

Lead in by asking a few students these questions:

Got any plans for the weekend?

What are you up to tonight?

Then have students work in pairs on the tasks here. Encourage them to record some of the complete expressions (e.g. *I'll probably stay in and take it easy. I suppose I might go travelling*) in their notebooks, perhaps under a section for the future. Finish up by asking students the same questions from the lead-in to see if they answer with different expressions.

Answers

The expressions in the dialogue are:

We'll probably take it easy this morning.

We might go to the Picasso exhibition.

Yeah, we're going to go up the Eiffel Tower this morning and then we're going to go for a cruise down the river.

Well, they said it's going to rain this morning, but it might clear up later.

Are you going to eat here tonight?

We might go out, it depends what time we get back this afternoon.

2 Practice

Students can do this exercise individually and then check their answers in pairs. Tell them to explain their decisions. Go over the pronunciation of these phrases, especially the contracted form *I'll* and the reduced pronunciation of *going to*. Then have students practise reading the conversations.

Answers

1. I'll, I might
2. I'm (just) going to, I might, I'll
3. we'll, we might
4. I might, I might, I'll
5. I'm going to
6. I'll, I might, I'm (not) going to

3 Further practice

This exercise gives students a chance to personalise these structures, and are good examples to include in their notebooks. Instead of having pairs of students just discuss these questions, have them wander around the class asking one question to one person before moving on to another person with another question. Finish up by asking the class who had the most interesting or unusual plans.

4 It depends

This is a very common phrase just by itself when we don't want to be explicit or when we want to delay answering. You could give students an example of an interaction like this:

A: *So, are you going to give us some homework tonight?*
B: *Well, it depends.*
A: *On what?*
A: *What kind of mood I'm in, I suppose.*

You might want to explain that *whether* and *if* are used when there is a choice, for example you're either on time or you're late. The words *or not* can therefore follow at the end of the sentence:
It depends if/whether I have time or not.

They can also follow directly after *whether* – but not *if*:
It depends whether or not I have time.

Answers

1. depends on	7. depends on	13. how long
2. depends on	8. depends	14. what time
3. depends	9. how	15. whether
4. depends	10. how much	16. what
5. depends on	11. what time	17. whether
6. depends	12. how	

5 Pronunciation: linking

This is sometimes a difficult concept for students to accept. Explain that not only will it help them speak more fluently in groups of words, but it will also help them to avoid the problem that some learners have of dropping certain final consonant sounds. Go through the two examples, and have students practise them before having them mark the linking in 1–9. Play the recording once all the way through and then again, pausing after each sentence so that students can repeat it several times. You can also point out that the 'd' sound is usually dropped in *it depends*.

Answers

9. It depends <u>how I</u> feel.
12. It depends how <u>tired I</u> am.
13. It depends how <u>long it'll</u> take.
14. It depends what <u>time I</u> get home.
15. It depends <u>whether I</u> get <u>back in</u> <u>time or</u> not.
16. It depends what <u>kind of</u> thing you like.
17. It depends <u>whether I've</u> got <u>paid or</u> not.

6 Further practice

Have students ask each other these questions in pairs and then ask them to spend a few minutes memorising the responses 1–8 in **4 It depends**. Then give each student a number from one to seven. This is the number of the question that they have to ask. Get all the students to stand up and go around asking their questions and trying to remember an appropriate response.

Answers

Possible answers:

1. It depends how I feel/how tired I am/what time I get home.

2. It depends how much time we've got/what time the film finishes.

3. It depends how I feel/how tired I am/what time I get home/whether I get back in time or not.

4. It depends how I feel/how tired I am/what time I get home.

5. It depends whether I've got paid or not.

6. It depends how long it'll take/how tired I am.

7. It depends how much time we've got.

7 Speaking

These pictures include some places that aren't typical tourist attractions. Explain what each place is. The pictures show Tokyo, Disneyland, The Hiroshima Peace Museum, and the Galapagos Islands. Write a few expressions on the board to help:

I'd never go there, even if you paid me.

It's not really the kind of thing I'm into.

I'm sure it's fascinating.

I think everyone should see it.

Follow-up

Have students choose one of the cities in the photographs on page 94 and imagine that they are on holiday there. They should write a letter or a postcard to a friend explaining what they have been doing, where they've been going, what they've been eating, how the weather has been, what the people have been like, etc. Give students a chance to review the language in this unit and previous ones. If you are having them write in class, go around helping. When they have finished, they can exchange letters with a partner, read it and then talk about it.

14 | Studying

Unit overview

General topic
Talking about schools and different kinds of exams and tests.

Reading
The way teachers used to discipline children in schools is not like it is now.

Language input

- Verb patterns: *She was caught drinking in school. She carried on driving even after her accident. He was sacked for always being late.* etc.

- School expressions: *He never pays attention in class. She's the teacher's pet.* etc.

- Expressions and collocations for talking about exams and tests: *I got my results. My mind went completely blank. I did a lot of revision for the exam.* etc.

- Intonation for expressing sympathy: *I'm <u>really</u> sorry to hear that. I'm <u>so</u> sorry.* etc.

- Verbs for talking about hopes and plans in the future: *I'm planning to spend the summer working abroad. I'm really looking forward to it.* etc.

- Asking opinions about the future and responding: *Do you think she'll come? I doubt it.*

- Pronunciation of the contracted form *'ll: It'll rain later. I'll give you a hand with it.*

Language strip

Use the language strip as a way to lead in to the unit. Ask students to look quickly through the list and find any expressions that they have used themselves (e.g. *Have you done your homework?*) and any that are true for them (e.g. *I hated school*). Explain that in this unit they will learn ways of talking about school and taking exams. Encourage them to choose some other expressions in the strip that look interesting and to find out more about them.

Use the language strip later on in this unit for a small group task. Ask students to find those expressions that are about exams (e.g. *I've got my results*), those that are about university (e.g. *I'm doing French at Nottingham*) and those that are about school (e.g. *How old were you when you left school?*). (Of course, some expressions do not fall into only one category.) You could then ask students to choose several of the expressions to ask each other (e.g. *What was your degree in again?*).

You might need to explain some of the following expressions:

- If you *drop out of university/school*, you leave without finishing. For example: *I got into a good university, but I just got fed up with it after a few months and dropped out.*

- If you are *doing a subject somewhere*, you are studying it. If it is at university and the university is named after the city, you can just use the city's name. For example: *I'm doing chemical engineering at Leeds.*

- If you are *having/taking a gap year*, you are taking a year off between leaving school and starting university. For example: *I'm planning to spend my gap year travelling around the world.*

- If *your mind goes blank*, you suddenly cannot remember or think of something. For example: *My mind's gone completely blank. I can't remember who gave me that necklace.*

- If you say *you got three As and a B*, you are referring to the results of your exams. Usually you are referring to your A-levels and the grades required to get into university. A-levels are exams that are usually taken in the final year of school in the UK when you are eighteen. *What do you call A-levels in your country?* means *What do you call the exams you take at the end of secondary school in your country?*

Remind students to record any of the expressions that they like in their notebooks.

Lead in

Lead in by writing the word *teacher* on the board. Then, as a class, brainstorm a list of adjective collocations. Here are some less obvious examples: *hardworking, overworked, competent, inexperienced, sympathetic.* Then go on to the first exercise.

Reading

1 Speaking

Introduce this exercise by telling students about some of your own teachers, for example a teacher that inspired you to become a teacher yourself, a teacher that made your life a misery, etc. If you are short of ideas, you can use this example:

A friend of mine once met one of her old teachers several years after she had left school. When she told her old teacher that she was herself a teacher, he nearly died of shock. Apparently, she had been quite unruly in school. When he asked what made her go into teaching, she explained that she had made her teachers' lives a misery as a student and now she wanted to make her students' lives a misery as a teacher!

Have students talk in pairs about the questions and the pictures on the page. Ask if any of the things in the pictures remind them of their own time at school.

2 While you read (The bad old days)

Point out the title of the article and ask students to guess what it might refer to. Then explain the task. Have students read through the article and then compare their answers with a partner.

> **Answers**
>
> Answers will vary.

Play the recording of the article while students follow in their Coursebook. Encourage them to underline any expressions or collocations that seem interesting. You may want to point out and explain the following expressions:

- If you voice *your support for someone/something*, you verbally express your support for that person or idea. We can use the verb *voice* with other emotions, too: *to voice your concern/anger/frustration*. For example: *A lot of people are voicing their frustration at the lack of progress in reaching an agreement.*
- If *you are at fault*, you are responsible for something that went wrong. For example: *The big food companies are really at fault for the problems of obesity.*
- If you are *cheeky*, you are being a little disrespectful and funny at the same time. For example: *I was cheeky towards the teachers, but I never got in really serious trouble.*
- If you *push someone to the limit*, you provoke them to a point where they lose control. For example: *You'd better stop now. You're pushing me to my limit.*
- If you *outlaw something*, you make it illegal. For example: *They've outlawed the use of mobile phones while driving.*

3 Speaking

Have students discuss these follow-up questions in small groups. You may want to point out the pattern *catch someone doing something*. The *-ing* form is used here because it shows that the action was in progress. Ask students for other things a teacher or the police might catch you doing. For example:
I was caught fighting in the toilets.
I was caught running in the corridors.
We were once caught shoplifting.

You could also explain that you can *skip meals*.
For example:
I usually skip breakfast.

Finish up by asking students who had the most unusual, effective or cruellest punishments. To extend the discussion, have students discuss whether it was right

that the teacher was sacked for grabbing the boy's shirt or whether physical punishment should be outlawed in schools and in the home.

4 Verb patterns

The verbs in this exercise are followed by a variety of patterns. This is a good time to make sure students are recording and learning examples in whole expressions. You may need to explain the difference between *blame somebody for a problem* and *blame a problem on a person*: *on* is followed by the cause, while *for* is followed by the result. Ask students to complete these sentences appropriately:
They blamed the crash on …
Whenever something got broken, it was always blamed on …
I blame the government for …
I always took the blame for …

> **Answers**
>
> 1. g.   2. f.   3. c.   4. a.   5. e.   6. d.   7. b.
>
> The expressions are:
> got sacked for tearing a boy's shirt
> complained to the headmaster
> sacked for physically abusing the boy
> caught two students talking in class
> make you hold your hands out like a cross
> carry on teaching the class
> caught anyone doing anything wrong
> threatening them with the sack
> blame the outlawing of physical punishment for an increase in bad behaviour in children
> get sacked for stopping a fight
> caught smoking in the toilets

5 Speaking

This exercise gives more practice with the verb patterns from **4 Verb patterns**. Have students look through the questions and then ask them to close their Coursebooks and ask you. Answer their questions and then ask them to recall several expressions you used. Write them on the board. Students can then open their books and discuss the questions themselves in small groups, using any of the expressions to help them if necessary.

6 Teachers and students

Here the focus is on several expressions connected to school. Students can work individually through the task and then compare answers with a partner. You could also ask them to decide which are positive and which are negative. As you go through the answers, check that they understand some of the expressions by asking further questions. For example:

How would a teacher know someone wasn't paying attention?

How would you know if I wasn't paying attention?

What kind of thing would you do if you were in detention?

What is the opposite of 'top of the class'?

How can a teacher be encouraging?

How could you tell someone was the 'teacher's pet'?

Then pairs of students can talk about the sentences that relate to their life.

Answers

Sentences concerning students: 1, 3, 5, 7, 9 and 11
Sentences concerning teachers: 2, 4, 6, 8, 10 and 12

Positive sentences: 2, 7 and 8.
The rest are negative.

Listening

1 Test, exam, degree, etc.

This exercise allows students to see the difference in meaning between similar words. To lead in, write *test*, *exam* and *degree* on the board. Ask students to use each word to write a sentence about themselves. Then have them do the exercise. When they have finished, ask them to look back at their sentences and modify the language if necessary, for example by changing or adding a collocation. Pairs of students can then talk about the qualifications they have or want to get. Write some more expressions with *qualification* on the board for students to complete and talk about:
I want to get a qualification in …
These days you need qualifications if you want to be a …
Most people who apply for … have got a lot of qualifications.

Answers

1. examination
2. degree, diploma, qualifications
3. certificate

---

2 Speaking

Introduce the task by discussing the initial questions with the class as a whole. Then have students individually decide the order and compare with a partner. Tell them to record the collocations that are new to them in their notebooks. Explain that if *you mess up something on a test*, you do it badly. If *you mess up your room*, however, you make it untidy. If *you manage to do something*, you are implying that it is difficult or requires some effort to accomplish. For example:
After five hours, I finally managed to get to the summit.

Answers

The correct order is:
1. c. 2. g. 3. d. 4. e. 5. a. 6. f. 7. h. 8. b.

---

3 Listening

Explain the situation and have students predict how the sentences will be completed. This helps reinforce some of the collocations from **2 Speaking**. Play the recording and then have students complete the sentences. Play it a second time for them to check. You can then have them listen a third time, following the tapescript on page 154.

Answers

1. fail, go to university
2. she only did one of the writing pieces
3. revised really hard for it, take the course and the exams again

---

4 Matching

Here are some more expressions about examinations. When students have finished doing the matching task, have them test each other in pairs, with one person saying the first half of the sentences and the other person completing it without looking at the Coursebook. Explain that if *you just about* or *barely scrape through an exam*, you only just pass it. For example:
You just about scraped through with 71%.

Answers

1. b. 2. e. 3. d. 4. f. 5. c. 6. a.

Expressions meaning the person did well: 2 and 3
Expressions meaning the person didn't do so well: 1, 4, 5 and 6

---

5 Pronunciation: intonation

Intonation conveys a lot of meaning. Write a simple sentence like *That's my book* on the board. Ask students to practise saying it with different emotions: anger, real pleasure, boredom, real pride, etc. Then ask them what they were doing with their voices to convey that emotion.

Play the recording once all the way through to allow students to hear the intonation patterns for the expressions giving sympathy. Play it a second time, pausing after each response to allow students to repeat. Then have them work in pairs reading the conversation. Have them think of ways to extend the dialogue. You might want to give an example with one student. For example:

A: I'm sorry I'm so late, but I had an accident in the car on the way here.

B: Oh, no! I'm sorry to hear that. Are you all right? What happened? Was the car badly damaged?

A: I'm fine, just a bit shaken. But the car's not in good shape. I had to get it towed to a garage.

B: So, did someone run into you or something?

A: Well, I'm to blame, really. I was trying to overtake this bus on a blind corner and I crashed right into this oncoming car.

Refer students to the **Real English** note on which words are stressed. Say a few sentences and have students practise, responding with the appropriate expression and intonation. For example:

I've lost that gold bracelet.

I've lost my pen.

I've lost a very dear friend.

Once students have practised their dialogues a few times, have them perform them to other pairs.

6 | I messed up badly!

This exercise features the topic of exams and tests with more connected expressions. Students can fill in the gaps and then check their answers in pairs. You could then read out 1–3 and either elicit the answers from the class as you come to each gap or else simply give the group the answers.

Answers			
1. a. revision	b. last	c. notes	d. failed
2. a. failed	b. Test	c. pass	d. enough.
3. a. cheating	b. confident	c. copied	d. well

Point out the expression *needless to say* in each story. This is a common way of ending a story when the result is what you would expect to happen. Give students a couple of expressions that might be used when the result is surprising. For example:

Funnily enough, (I passed).

Imagine my surprise when I found out (I'd passed).

Students might want to use some of these expressions to end their own exam stories. Let students spend a few minutes looking back through the previous exercises before telling their stories again to their partner.

If you want to revise the language in these three stories in a later lesson, one way you could do it is to write a few key words from each story on the board and put students in groups to re-tell the stories. For example, you could write up the following:

1. left his revision / most of the time … but one night / stayed up all night / several caffeine tablets / Unfortunately, / Needless to say, …

2. my driving test / halfway through / for ages / started waving / the car in front of me / crashed / Needless to say, …

3. A friend of mine / copying / cheating / one of the best students in the school / confident / Unfortunately, / Needless to say, …

You could round up by re-telling the stories yourself, eliciting as many of the collocations and expressions from the class as you can – or else you could simply ask them to compare the versions they have thought of – or written – with those on page 100.

7 | Speaking

Start off by asking students to sort the tests and exams in the box according to different criteria, for example, those that you revise for, those that you don't like, those with serious consequences if you fail, etc. You might need to explain that *a screen test* is for an actor who wants a part in a film, and that *a mock exam* is a practice exam.

After students have told their partner a story, have them tell the same story to another person.

Using grammar

1 | The future: seven important verbs

Remind students that the structures *I'm going to, I'll probably* and *I might* from Unit 13 express how certain we feel about things in the future.

This exercise will help students with the general meaning of the seven verbs and the grammatical patterns that follow them. Have students sort the expressions into categories: those that are followed by an infinitive with *to* (e.g. *plan, hope, expect*), those followed by a preposition + a noun or *-ing* form (e.g. *think of, look forward to*) and those followed by a noun (e.g. *apply for, dread, expect*).

Answers	
1. apply	5. think
2. dread	6. look forward to
3. plan	7. expect, expect
4. hope	

2 | Practice

Before doing this exercise, make sure students are comfortable with the formation of the present continuous as well as the spelling guidelines for when to double the consonant (e.g. *plan –planning*) and dropping the final 'e' (e.g. *hope – hoping*).

Answers

1. a. 'm expecting	b. 'm (not) expecting
2. a. 'm applying	b. 'm applying
3. a. 'm (really) looking forward to	b. 'm (really) looking forward to
4. a. 'm hoping	b. 'm hoping
5. a. 'm planning	b. 'm (not) planning
6. a. 'm thinking	b. 'm thinking
7. a. 'm dreading	b. 'm dreading

You may need to explain that *PR* stands for *public relations*. Tell students some examples about yourself or a friend before having them do the same in pairs.

3 | Asking for an opinion

This exercise focuses on the very common question *Do you think + will … ?* Go over the explanation and then have students put the words in the right order to make questions. Students shouldn't find it too difficult because they all start with *Do you think … ?* Play the recording so students can check their answers, and then play it again, pausing after each question so that they can repeat.

Answers

1. Do you think she'll come?
2. Do you think I'll need a coat?
3. Do you think you'll see Ken later?
4. Do you think we'll be back by eight?
5. Do you think you'll pass?
6. Do you think you'll do a Master's after you graduate?

4 | Short natural answers

Lead in by having students ask you some *Do you think … ?* opinion questions about the future. Answer, using some of the short answers here. Then go over the explanations. These short expressions are very common, and in this context are more typical than responses with modal auxiliaries like *must* and *may* for expressing degrees of certainty in the future, something which some students might ask about.

Answers

1. a. I doubt it   b. It's bound to   c. It might
2. a. hopefully   b. definitely   c. probably
3. a. Definitely   b. I doubt it   c. hopefully

If students don't know, Lazio and Arsenal are football teams from Rome and London respectively. In dialogue number 3, note the expression *her parents are going to kill me*. You might say *someone is going to kill me* to mean that they are going to be very angry when they find out about something you have done or not done.

5 | Write a conversation

Have students work in pairs creating the dialogues. Then have them practise reading them a few times. You could suggest that they memorise two or three and then perform them for another pair.

6 | Pronunciation: *'ll*

This contraction is a little difficult for some speakers. You may need to have students practise this exercise several times. Play the recording once all the way through and then again, pausing after each sentence. For extra practice, ask students to choose five of the responses and write the accompanying question. They can then ask their questions to a partner who chooses the appropriate response. You may need to explain that if you *give someone a hand*, you help them do something. For example:

A: *I'm having trouble fixing my fence.*

B: *I'll come over and give you a hand if you like.*

7 | Free practice

In this exercise, encourage students to make a follow-up comment as well. For example:

A: *What do you think the weather will be like tomorrow?*

B: *It's bound to rain. It's the weekend. It always rains at the weekend here.*

As an alternative, write these questions on slips of paper and give one to each student. They then go around the class and ask their question to another student. When they have finished, they exchange slips and find someone else to ask their new question to, and so on.

15 Sport

Unit overview

General topic
Talking about sport and making predictions.

Listening
Five people talk about sporting events.

Language input

- Verb collocations with various sports: *I play a bit of golf now and then. I go swimming quite a lot, golf course, basketball court*, etc.
- Expressions to talk about keeping fit: *I do like to keep fit. I avoid red meat.* etc.
- Vocabulary for describing sporting events: *it was a dirty game, it's an away game, the fight was fixed*, etc.
- First conditionals: *If they score first, they'll have a chance. If he doesn't have any mechanical problems, he should win.*
- Common *if*- expressions: *I'll come if I can. I'll give you a hand if you want.*
- Agreeing, disagreeing and showing surprise with *know*: *I know! I mean how much does Tiger Woods earn a year? I don't know. I thinks she's quite sexy. I don't know why she stays with him.* etc.

Language strip

Use the language strip as a way to lead in to the unit. Ask students to quickly look through the list and find at least two expressions that they could see themselves using. Explain that in this unit they will learn more ways of talking about sport. Encourage them to choose some other expressions in the strip that look interesting and to find out more about them.

Use the language strip later on in this unit for a small group task. Ask students to discuss which sport is being referred to in some of the expressions. You could also ask them to find expressions that might be said about a sport that you are watching or have just finished watching (e.g. *He should have been sent off*).

You might need to explain some of the following expressions.

- If a team are playing *at home*, they are playing at their own ground or stadium. For example: *Why do they always play so badly at home?*
- In some team sports, like football, *a player is sent off* if the referee decides that they have seriously broken one of the rules of the game. For example: *I can't believe he was sent off for that tackle.*

- *Kilmarnock* is a Scottish football team.
- In some sports like tennis, if you are *the number one seed*, you are ranked as the best player in a competition. For example: *She stands a good chance now that the number one seed is out.*
- *It's a par 5* refers to golf. It means that five hits of the ball are expected on this one particular hole.
- *The dogs* refers to dog racing.
- *Game, set and match* could be said when a player wins a tennis match. This means that a player has just won the last game of a set, the last set, and the match itself.
- If you say *It was out*, you are usually referring to the fact that the ball has gone out of play. For example, in cricket you would say *It was out* if you believe that the batsman is out. This expression is also used when the ball has landed outside the line during a tennis match. Fans watching a match or game will use this expression when they disagree with the umpire or referee's decision that it wasn't out.
- *A shuttlecock* is the object that players hit over the net in badminton.
- *We got thrashed* means we lost a game/match very heavily.
- *He's got a great left foot* is usually said about a footballer and means he's very skilful with his left foot.

Remind students to record any of the expressions that they like in their notebooks.

Lead in

Get students into pairs. Give them one minute to write down all the sports they can think of; however, one person has to write down all the team sports while the other person all the individual sports. After one minute, students can compare to see who had the most. Then, as a class, get students to tell you the sports in their lists, while you write them on the board. Refer students to the pictures on page 104 to see if any of the sports they came up with are shown. Keep the list on the board while students do **1 Are you any good?**.

Using vocabulary

1 Are you any good?

Here students sort the sports according to whether they collocate with *play* or *go*. When they have finished, ask if they notice any patterns. They may tell you that the sports with *ball* in them tend to collocate with *play* and those ending with -ing tend to collocate with go. Get students to look at the list of sports on the board and decide if they collocate with go or play. You might have some like boxing and tae-kwon do that collocate with do. Point out the expressions a lot of, quite a lot, a bit of, almost every day, sometimes, now and then. Ask which of them mean that the person does a sport frequently.

Answers

1. go 2. play 3. play 4. go 5. go 6. play 7. play
8. play 9. go 10 go.

Students should match the follow-up comments in pairs, using a dictionary or asking you when necessary about any of the sport-related vocabulary. (The best way to explain some of the expressions like dribbling is by miming the action.) After checking the answers, ask students what patterns they notice and write the following on the board:
I'm quite good at + -ing.
I'm OK at + -ing.
I'm not very good at + -ing.

Model the example dialogue with one student, pointing out the intonation pattern of Oh, really? before having students talk about some of the sports in pairs.

Answers

1. i. 2. b. 3. a. 4. e. 5. h. 6. f. 7. j. 8. c.
9. g. 10. d.

2 Where do you play?

This exercise focuses on the names for the places where sports are played. If you want to extend this, you can brainstorm other names like ice-hockey rink, cricket ground, athletics track, bowling alley, etc. Once students have done the matching task, model the example dialogue before getting them to work in pairs. Point out that the expression Do you know if there's anywhere I can ... ? is useful for other places. For example:
Do you know if there's anywhere I can buy a stamp/make a photocopy round here?

Answers

1. b. 2. c. 3. a. 4. a. 5. b. 6. a. 7. a. 8. a.
9. b. 10. d.

3 Keeping fit

Lead in by asking students a few questions. For example:
What do you do to keep fit?
How often do you get some physical exercise?
What do you eat if you want to have a healthy diet?

Before getting students to read the text, put the following words and phrases on the board: fruit and vegetables, yoga, team sports, red meat, stamina, gym. Ask students to predict what might be said about each one in a text about keeping fit. For example:
It's a good idea to do yoga.
You shouldn't eat red meat.

You may need to explain that if you have stamina, you are able to do something for a long time. For example:
You need a lot of stamina to do cross-country running.

Then have students read the text and complete the gaps. Before going through the answers, ask what they think have a go at means (try).

Answers

1. team sports
2. aggressive
3. going on about
4. keep fit
5. red meat
6. fruit and vegetables
7. gym
8. yoga
9. stamina
10. have a go at

If you wish, you could ask students to change any of the expressions a little to make them true. For example:
The one thing I would like to have a go at is ice-hockey.

You may need to explain that if your body is supple, you can bend and move it easily, while if it is stiff, you can't; and that we can use the expression I watch what I eat to mean that we try to have a healthy diet by being careful about the foods we choose to eat. Encourage students to record in their notebooks some of the expressions in the text, particularly the ones that describe themselves.

4 Describing an event

This exercise introduces some more sporting vocabulary. Have students work in pairs on the matching task. Then, as a class, discuss which sport is being described, explaining how the expressions are typical for that particular sport. If some students need help with any of the terms here like sets or yellow cards, ask if there is anyone in the class who can explain. There usually is someone who knows what these terms mean.

Answers

1. f. (golf: the greens)
2. c. (football: teams, grounds)
3. d. (for example, tennis, football: match, final)
4. h. (football: away game)
5. e. (boxing: fight)
6. b. (skiing: downhill, slope, icy)
7. g. (football: sent off, yellow cards)
8. a. (tennis: sets)

As an extension, ask pairs of students to come up with some expressions to describe an event in one of the sports pictured on page 104 or 105. For example for cycling, you could say *the conditions were perfect.* You could also bring in various sports reports from newspapers or the Internet for students to read and underline the associated expressions.

5 | Speaking

Students can discuss these questions in small groups. Go around monitoring and collecting examples of any language students are having problems with – as well as any good uses of language – to give feedback on when they have finished. Follow up by getting students to close their Coursebooks and ask you the questions. For example:

A: *Have you heard of any matches being fixed?*

B: *Well, wasn't it rumoured that the 1998 World Cup Final was fixed? I mean, how else could you explain Brazil's performance?*

Using grammar

1 | First conditionals

In this section students focus on the structure often called the first conditional. The structure is typified by the use of the word *if* to introduce the condition – often in a clause – and a clause referring to a possible result. Students may have studied that the clause with the result uses *will*. Although *will* is frequent, remind students that we use various structures to talk about the future, and so other modal auxiliaries are common in first conditional expressions too.

Lead in by asking a question about an up-coming game the class will be familiar with. For example:

Do you think ... will be a good game?

Do you think ... will win?

Then have students complete the task. As you go through the answers, ask which sport is being discussed. You might need to explain that *Michael Owen* is an English football player and *Rangers* are a football team from Glasgow.

Answers

1. d. (athletics: race, sprint finish)
2. c. (football)
3. a. (football: score)
4. b. (tennis: serve, double faults)
5. e. (motor racing: mechanical problems, breaks down)
6. f. (any team sport: they play, they win)

Point out several expressions here with the verb *have*: *have an off day, have a chance* and *have problems.* For *have an off day,* give the class some other examples, such as: *I'm sorry about that, I'm having a bit of an off day today.*

You could also give them variations of this pattern: *I'm having a good/bad/hell of a day.*

Ask students what kind of day they are having. Also, point out the collocations here. For example: *score first, have a chance, serves well, gives away double faults, sprint finish.*

Go over the grammar explanation with students and make sure they notice the use of the present simple in the *if* clause. Also, explain that *then* is used to emphasise the conditional relationship between the two actions. Then ask students to notice the different modal expressions in the main clause. Explain that they indicate different feelings about the future. For example, *should* shows that we expect it to happen, while *could possibly* and *might* show that we aren't so sure as *'ll probably.* Draw students' attention to the fact that we say *'ll probably/definitely,* but *probably/definitely won't.*

2 | Further practice

Students can now apply the guidelines or rules they established in **1 First conditionals** to the context of reporting news. Get students to do this exercise individually before having them check their answers in pairs. Encourage them to use some of the modal auxiliary phrases from **1 First conditionals**. Go around the class, checking their answers as they work. Then play the recording so that they can compare. Point out some of the expressions in the task and ask further questions. For example:

What else, apart from 'talks' can break down? (a car, a marriage)

What's the opposite of 'put up taxes'? (lower/reduce/cut taxes)

What happens when there's a famine? (crops die, harvests fail, people starve to death)

What else could you be thinking of 'going on'? (a cruise, a holiday, a strike)

What happens when a company is taken over?

Before having students practise reading the conversations in pairs, do the first one as an example, to show how the conversation can be continued.

3 Free practice

Have students write four or five questions and answers, and then have them wander around the class asking their questions. Give them an example of a possible conversation:

A: *Do you think Brazil will win the next World Cup?*

B: *It depends. If they play like they did in the last one, then they'll definitely stand a chance.*

A: *Do you really think so? I think if they come up against Germany again, they'll definitely lose.*

Have students speak to several people. You might also want to take part in this activity as students will be able to hear the language you use and perhaps re-use it themselves.

4 Role play

Give students a few minutes to think about what they want to say about each person and how they want to say it. Get them to role-play the dialogue in pairs before changing partners and repeating the task with someone new. You might want to point out the gossiping expressions:

Have you heard that … ?

Did you know that … ?

Did … tell you that … ?

I heard that …

Someone told me that …

Students can then use them to have a quick gossip about some people they know.

5 *If-* clauses

Get students to complete the expressions, and then play the recording so they can check their answers. Then play the recording again, pausing after each sentence, so the students can repeat. Then get pairs of students to discuss in what situation you might use some of these expressions. For example, *I'll come if I can* could be a response to an invitation to a party. Encourage students to remember these common expressions as whole phrases. After they have finished this exercise, write the first two words of each expression (e.g. *I'll give*) on the board, and students can see if they can complete them from memory.

Listening

1 Speaking

Students can discuss these questions as a whole class or in small groups. You could also have them discuss whether it is better to watch something live or on TV, and whether it depends on the sport. Write some useful expressions on the board. For example:

You can't beat the atmosphere.

You don't get a very good view.

You spend a fortune to get soaking wet looking at the back of someone's head.

2 People talking about sport

Explain the situation and play the recording. Get students to answer the questions in both tasks and then to discuss their answers in pairs. Explain that if something is *controversial*, there is a lot of debate about it. For example, we can talk about *controversial decisions, policies, books, films.* Also, explain the more informal expressions:

- If *someone/a team is thrashed*, they lose heavily.

- If you *blow it*, you had a chance of doing something successfully, but lost the chance.

3 | I know!

This exercise introduces an expression for agreeing that is a more normal alternative to *I agree*. Model the examples for the students and point out the use of the discourse marker *I mean* to introduce a statement that explains the reason for your agreement. Before students talk about the statements 1–5 with a partner, model an example with one of the students:

A: *There's too much sport on TV these days.*

B: *I know. I mean, a whole afternoon of golf on a Sunday afternoon. It's ridiculous.*

You may need to explain that if you think *something is pointless*, you don't think it is worthwhile because you don't see its purpose. We can talk about *a pointless discussion* or *meeting* and say that *it is/seems pointless to do something*. For example:
It seems absolutely pointless to carry on like this.

Answers

The five examples from the tapescript on page 156 are:
I know. Five—one up in the last set and serving for the match – he should've won.

I know. He just seemed to go to pieces.

I know. It was awful.

I know. They must've bribed the judges or something.

I know. I just don't know how they can say Winton won on points.

For 1–5, answers will vary.

---

4 | I don't know

Here students see another functional use of an expression with *know*. Go over the example and the explanation with students, before having them do the matching task. Then explain the second task. Point out that *I don't know* expresses slight disagreement here. Play the recording so that students can check their answers. You may want to explain that we often say that *a washing machine eats our socks* to explain the strange phenomenon of how socks seem to disappear in a washing machine!

Answers

1. d. vi.   2. f. iv.   3. e. iii.   4. a. ii.   5. c. i.   6. b. v.

---

5 | Pronunciation: intonation

Play the recording of the conversations in **2 People talking about sport** and **4 I don't know** again, so that students can hear the rising intonation pattern of *I don't know* and the flatter intonation of *I know*. Then have them practise the conversations in pairs.

6 | Speaking

Instead of having students work in pairs on this exercise, you can have them stand up and go around the class, asking one question to one person before asking another question to someone else. Have them speak to about eight people if possible, so that they get to practise each question twice.

7 | And finally

Before students work on this, make sure they know what each of these sports are. You may need to explain the following:

- *Curling* is a winter sport where you slide a large circular stone down an ice sheet towards a target area.

- *Synchronised swimming* is like ballet in the water, and the participants have to perform movements in perfect time with each other.

Then get students to work in pairs sorting the sports into the three categories. When they have finished, they can compare their decisions with another group.

Follow-up

To tie in with the topic from the previous unit, ask students what they remember about playing sport in school. Write some expressions on the board to help them, and then get them to talk about their answers with a partner:

I was quite good at ... when I was younger.

I really used to look forward to ...

I used to really hate ...

We had this really (adjective) games/physical education teacher ...

I used to be on the ... team.

I never made it on to the ... team because ...

I played ... for my school.

I represented my school at ...

Unit overview

General topic
Talking about business and politics.

Reading
A Chinese-Indonesian built up his own business from nothing.

Language input

- Business collocations: *employ lots of people, make contacts, runs his own business,* etc.

- Expressions with *business* and *company: We do a lot of business in South Korea and Taiwan. It's against company policy.* etc.

- Collocations and expressions with *money: it's good value for money, owe money to the bank,* etc.

- Collocations with *market: corner the market, flood the market, the market is booming,* etc.

- Business verbs: *launch a product, promote a product, set prices, raise prices,* etc.

- Second conditionals: *The government could invest more money in schools if they wanted to. If it was mine, I'd lend it to you.*

Language strip

Use the language strip as a way to lead in to the unit. Ask students to quickly look through the list and find any expressions that could be said about their country or about a company they work for. Explain that in this unit they will learn ways of talking about the world of business. Encourage them to choose some other expressions in the language strip that look interesting and to find out more about them.

Use the language strip later on in this unit for a small group task. Ask students to find those expressions that are about the economy (e.g. *The housing market is booming*) and those said about a company (e.g. *It's an old family business*). Then ask them to discuss what *it* or *they* might be referring to in some of the expressions.

You might need to explain some of the following expressions.

- If *you have built up a company from nothing,* you started with a very small company and little money and have turned it into a much bigger one. For example: *It's a real shame that they are selling the business off; she built it up from nothing.*

- If you refer to something as a *widget,* you mean it is a small object/bit of equipment that you don't know the name of. For example: *The beer stays fresher for longer now, because they put a widget in the can.*

- If *a market is booming,* there is a lot of buying and selling going on. We can also describe *the economy* as *booming.* For example: *The prime minister's chances of being re-elected are looking good, with low unemployment and a booming economy.*

- If you say *someone could sell fridges to Eskimos,* you are implying that they are so good at selling things that they would be able to sell something to a person who neither needs it nor wants it.

- If you *deal with customers,* you have a job that involves working with people who want to buy goods or service from you. For example: *I'm looking for a position where I don't have to deal with customers all the time.*

- If a company *went to the wall,* they went bankrupt.

Remind students to record any of the expressions that they like in their notebooks.

Lead in

Ask students if they are in business, or would ever consider going into business, and to think about what the advantages and disadvantages are of running your own business. This leads in nicely to the first exercise.

Reading

1 Speaking

You can use the questions in the first task for a whole class discussion. Then point out the collocation *face problems* – perhaps mentioning some other verb collocations, such as *deal with problems, solve problems, get round problems* – before having students work in pairs discussing the problems 1–8 in the second task. You may also need to explain that *bureaucracy* refers to a system with a lot of complicated and annoying rules, and is usually used negatively. Other words that collocate with *bureaucracy* are *eliminate* and *cut* (i.e. *eliminate bureaucracy* and *cut bureaucracy*).

Before moving on to the reading task in the next exercise, get students to tell you who they think would be good at dealing with most of the items 1–8.

2 | While you read (A self-made man)

Introduce the reading task by referring students to the pictures on pages 110 and 111. Ask students what they think the article is going to be about, based on what they see in the pictures. Encourage the use of structures like:
It's probably about how …
It might have something to do with when …
It could be connected with …

Then go over the introduction and explain the task. Have students read the article without worrying about understanding everything. They can then compare their answers with a partner. Ask them to explain the title *A self-made man*.

Answers

The problems mentioned in the article are:

dealing with employees (1 Speaking, number 1)

dealing with officials and bureaucracy (1 Speaking, number 2)

raising the money to start a business (1 Speaking, number 4)

selling things (1 Speaking, number 7)

making contacts (1 Speaking, number 8)

Other problems he mentions are:
living away from his family
paying taxes and wages
meeting deadlines
having his shops attacked in anti-Chinese rioting
dealing with corruption and an unstable economy
deciding who is going to take over the company

Play the recording of the article as students follow in the Coursebook. Encourage them to underline any interesting expressions and collocations. You may want to point out the following, which aren't dealt with in later exercises:

- If you describe a place as being *in the middle of nowhere*, it is far away from other places. For example: *I was dropped off in the middle of nowhere and had to walk miles to the nearest village.*

- You say *on top of all that* when you are listing negative things and want to add yet another one to the list. For example: *I got soaking wet on my way to work, my computer wouldn't start up, and on top of all that, the boss wanted to see me about the contract we had just lost.*

- If you describe someone as *soft*, you mean that they aren't tough or strict enough to do something. For example: *I had this really soft teacher at school. He let the kids get away with everything.*

3 | Useful collocations

This exercise focuses on several verb + noun collocations that appear in the text. Students can work on the tasks individually and then compare with a partner how the collocations were used in the text. Follow up with students testing each other in pairs, with one person saying the verb and the other person trying to remember the noun phrase that collocates with it. Encourage students to record the collocations and the examples from the text that they want to remember in their notebooks. In another follow-up activity, you could even have students put the collocations in the order that they occur in the text, and then use them to recall as much of the story as they can.

Answers

1. d.   2. c.   3. a.   4. e.   5. b.   6. j.   7. h.   8. f.
9. i.   10. g

---

4 | Speaking

These questions follow on from some of the issues raised in the article **A self-made man**. Have small groups of students discuss them as you go around the class monitoring. You may want to lead in by talking about the first two questions yourself to give students some ideas. To follow up, you could have pairs of students write a conversation between Darno and his son, in which Darno explains how life was much harder when he was young. This would be a good opportunity to revise comparative structures and to see how students use the structure *used to* which is focused on in the next unit. Write some expressions that students might find useful. For example:
In my day, we used to …
Young people today don't know what hard work is.
I'm sure it wasn't as bad as all that!
At least you could get a job!

5 | Business, company

Here students can again focus on the difference between two similar words by looking at their collocations. Encourage students to devote a page in their notebooks to expressions using these two words. As you go through the answers, ask further questions to help reinforce the language. For example:
Why do you think it's called a company car? (The company buys it for the employee and keeps it if the employee leaves.)

What might be some other things that are against company policy? (smoking in offices, personal use of e-mail)

How could a strong currency cause a company to lose business? (It is more expensive for customers in other countries to buy your products.) And what happens to companies if the currency is weak?

You could ask if students notice that in the examples here *company* refers to a particular organisation.

> **Answers**
>
> 1. company 2. business 3. company 4. business
> 5. business 6. company 7. business 8. company

You may need to explain the two idiomatic expressions. We can sometimes use *business* to refer to an event or situation, especially if it is topical. *Company* sometimes refers to other people who are with you, so if *you keep someone company*, you are with them to stop them feeling lonely. Here are some other idiomatic expressions with these two words:
It's none of your business.
Mind your own business.
This means business.
We've got company.
We parted company years ago.
You're in good company.

Using vocabulary

1 Talking about money

Students can work individually on this exercise and then discuss the last two questions with a partner. Follow up by asking pairs of students to tell you their suggestions of when to use these phrases so that you can check their understanding.

> **Answers**
>
> 1. value 2. waste 3. got 4. short 5. burn
> 6. married
>
> Possible answers for when you might use the sentences:
> 1. You might use this sentence in a restaurant which serves large portions but is quite cheap.
> 2. You might use this sentence if someone wanted to buy a first-class rail ticket for a twenty-minute train ride.
> 3. You might use this sentence to your partner if you want to buy something and you don't have enough money with you.
> 4. You might use this sentence if someone asks if you could lend them some money but you don't have any money to lend them, or if you don't want to lend them any money.
> 5. You might use this sentence if someone has spent more money on something than you think they should have.
> 6. You might use this sentence if you think that the only reason a woman has married a man is because he is rich.

2 Verb + *money*

Here are more collocations with *money*. Remember to focus students' attention on the prepositions too. Get students in pairs and ask them to think of another way to complete each phrase. For example:
borrow money from my parents
invest money in the stock market

Encourage them to record these expressions in their notebooks. As you go through the answers, you might want to ask further questions which aren't discussed later in **4 Speaking**. For example:
How else could you save money on holiday?
Where's the best place to invest your own money these days?
What could be some examples of stupid things you don't really need?

Ask students why they might want to borrow money from a friend, to elicit purpose expressions with *to*. For example:
To buy a coffee.
To pay my parents back.

> **Answers**
>
> 1. d. 2. c. 3. a. 4. b. 5. h. 6. g. 7. f. 8. e.

3 Further practice

This exercise gives students an opportunity to see these collocations used in context. You may want to spend some time reviewing the difference between *borrow* and *lend*. Explain that *to borrow* is to receive something temporarily, while *to lend* is to give something temporarily. Encourage students to record example sentences using these verbs in their notebooks, especially ones that they might use themselves a lot. For example:
Can I borrow your dictionary for a minute?

You may want to point out some other collocations and expressions in this exercise:
take out a loan
it's worth over twenty-five thousand pounds
before we set off
has more money than sense

You may need to explain that if you *get a tax break*, the amount of tax you have to pay is reduced because you belong to a certain category of tax-payer, for example, you are a parent. Or you may get your taxes reduced because you have done something with your money which entitles you to a reduction, for example, you have given some of it to charity.

> **Answers**
>
> 1. owe 2. invest 3. change 4. wastes 5. gave
> 6. spend 7. lend 8. borrow 9. borrowed 10. lent

Finish up by discussing the questions at the end of the exercise as a class. It might also be interesting to explore how the collocations of *money* and *time* are similar in English. Ask students to think of words or phrases that collocate with both nouns. For example: *waste, save, run out of, invest, short of* + *time/money*. You can then teach students the expression *time is money*. Ask if *time* has similar collocations in their own language and if not, whether there is another noun that does.

Incidentally, the saying *Neither a lender nor a borrower be* is from Shakespeare's *Hamlet*.

4 Speaking

This exercise gives students an opportunity to use some of the language from the previous exercises. The topic of charity might be one to explore further. You could have groups discuss questions like:
What are some big charitable organisations in your country?

What do you think the most deserving charitable causes are?

Is it right that people get tax breaks for giving to charity? Shouldn't they just be taxed more?

Do some charities do more harm than good?

You could also ask students to discuss when the following expressions might be used:
All proceeds go to charity.
It's for a good cause.
I don't accept charity!

5 Collocations with *market*

In the next two exercises, students focus on another word that has many collocations, a lot of which are idiomatic. Remind students, therefore, to include a translation along with those expressions that they record in their notebooks. Discuss the question about how Darno Setiadi cornered the propeller market by getting someone in the government to help him get an import licence before having students find the collocations in the text.

Answers

Collocations with *market*:
a fairly closed market
open up the market
make the market more competitive
break into the market
dominate the market
totally squeezed out of the market
cornered the market
the black market
flood the market

Have pairs of students talk about anything in the text that is also true about their own country. You could also ask them to use each of the collocations to write a true sentence about their own country. For example:
We've been forced to open up our rice market.

6 Talking about markets

While the main focus in **5 Collocations with *market*** was on verb collocations, here it is on adjective collocations. Draw students' attention to the words and phrases in the box, and point out that those on the right are positive, while those on the right are negative. You may need to explain the following:
- If *a market is saturated*, the market cannot grow any more, because the supply of products exceeds demand.
- *Do-it-yourself* refers to home improvements that you do yourself.

If you are from a different country from your students, have them ask you some questions about the markets there. For example:
What's the … market like in … these days?

7 Business verbs

Have students work in pairs to discuss the questions. Encourage them to use a dictionary or to ask you if they have questions about meaning. Go over the questions again, having the students share their answers with the whole class.

Answers

Possible answers:
1. They discover the product is a health hazard or could cause accidents somehow; they discover a design fault.
2. Because a new advertising strategy is very unpopular; because protesters boycott the product due to the fact it is made in cheap south-east Asian factories, etc.

   British Airways always used to have the British flag – the Union Jack – on the tailfins of their planes. They decided to replace them with a more global range of designs. This proved to be very unpopular, so they had to rethink their strategy. In the end, they went back to the old design. It was a very costly mistake!
3. To take control of a larger share of the market; to kill off the competition; to acquire new products / markets, etc.
4. To cover increasing production costs; to increase profits.
5. To pass on the benefits of decreased production costs to customers; to attract attention to their brand; to sell off old or unwanted stock, etc.
6. Senior managers leaving and starting to work for one of the main competitors; fraud; an economic collapse, etc.
7. Being caught stealing from the company you work for; a sex scandal; being accused of sexism/racism/harassment, etc.

8. They've just had a child; they want to travel for a year; one of their parents is ill, etc.

9. Because they are incompetent; because they undermine the boss's authority; because they are always late, etc.

Using grammar

1 Listen

The listening task contains several examples of the second conditional, which is the focus of **2 Second conditionals**. Introduce the listening task by having students talk about their own views of politicians. You might want to provide students with some collocations either before or after they do this. For example:
He/she's a clever/respected/shrewd/politician.
Most politicians are honest/dishonest/power-hungry/criminals/fairly decent people.

Play the recording and then have students discuss their answers in pairs. Then ask if they can remember the politician collocations they heard in the dialogue –
They're all liars, I just don't trust any of them, they're all corrupt, They're all only interested in making money for themselves – and add them to the list on the board. Play the recording again as the class follows the tapescript on page 156. Point out the structure Miriam uses:
They're all ... . This is common when we want to make generalisations.

Answers

Bob is probably going to vote for the People's Workers' Party because he thinks that if they were in power, they would be able to reduce unemployment by running things like the railways and the telephones, and make big business and the wealthy pay more taxes, which the party would invest in schools and hospitals.

Miriam is probably not going to vote. She thinks politicians are all liars, corrupt, and they are all equally bad; they are only interested in making money for themselves. She doesn't trust any of them. They all say the same thing and have the same policies.

2 Second conditionals

In this exercise students are encouraged to develop a 'guideline' for the use of second conditionals before reading the explanation. After they read the explanation, you may want to talk a little about how in English the past tense doesn't always refer to time. Sometimes it expresses distance, either in terms of politeness and respect (e.g. *I wanted to ask you something*) or, as in the case here, distance from reality i.e., what we don't expect to happen. Remind students that in the previous

unit they looked at first conditional structures, many of which used *will*. We can think of *would* as a 'past' form of *will*.

Point out the variety of modal auxiliaries that are found in the main result clause of second conditionals. Some students may wonder if *were* should be used instead of *was*. Although *were* is perfectly acceptable, it is considered more formal and is becoming less common than *was* in spoken English.

Answers

1. Bob thinks the government make big business and rich people pay higher taxes.
2. The government are actually cutting taxes.
3. He uses the 'past tense' and *would* to show that he doesn't think it will happen.

Other examples of second conditionals in the tapescript are:
If the state was running things like the railways and telephones, we wouldn't have such high levels of unemployment.
If they taxed business more, then they'd just go somewhere else, or find some way of avoiding paying it.

3 Practice

This exercise contains some common second conditional expressions and patterns: For example:
... could ... if they wanted to
people just wouldn't accept it

Encourage students to record these in their notebooks. Point out that the phrase *that way* is used to introduce the consequence of the previous statement i.e., *if they/you did that*.

Answers

1. could, wanted to, did, 'd
2. wouldn't, did, would, 'd
3. could, did, would, would
4. did, might, 'd
5. did, wouldn't, 'd
6. would, 'd, wouldn't

One thing you could do before having pairs of students discuss the opinions in dialogues 1–6, is to review the *I know* and *I don't know* structures on page 108 in the previous unit. They can then practise having conversations like this:
A: *I think they should ban smoking, at least in public places.*
B: *I know. I mean, that way, they'd save a lot of money on medical bills.*
A: *Personally, I think that the government could invest more in schools if they wanted to.*
B: *I don't know. It's not as simple as all that.*

4 | Refusing requests

Refusing requests is another common use of second conditionals. Lead in by asking the students to think of a request to make to you. When they ask, turn them down, using second conditionals. For example:

A: *Can you not give us any homework tonight?*

B: *You know, if I could, I would, but I've got to give you some every day.*

After answering a request, ask if students can recall what you said, and write the expressions on the board. Then go over the explanation in the Coursebook and do the tasks.

> **Answers**
>
> 1. g.   2. d.   3. c.   4. f.   5. a.   6. b.   7. e.
>
> Possible questions:
>
> 2. Do you fancy coming with us to Paris next weekend?
>
> 3. Do you want to come out for a drink after work?
>
> 4. A new club's opened up and a group of us from work are going down to see what it's like. Do you want to join us?
>
> 5. Would it be OK if I stayed at your place?
>
> 6. Is it all right if the band come round to practise tonight?
>
> 7. I couldn't borrow Freddie's car for the day, could I?

5 | Free practice

In this task most of the examples of the second conditional are about hypothetical present situations, rather than what we don't expect to happen. For example:

I'm a man, but if I were a woman, I'd …

Point out that the expression *if I had the money/time* means *if I had enough money/time to do something*. Have students complete these sentence starters, and then talk about them in small groups. To turn the task into a game, have pairs of students write how they think you would complete the sentences. Then tell the class your ideas. Students get one point for each correct prediction.

Follow-up

Ask students to work in pairs and imagine that they are CEOs of a big high-profile company like Starbucks, McDonald's, Microsoft, Shell, etc. They should then think of how they would do business differently, what changes they would make, what new markets they would seek to break into, etc. Give them the beginning:

If we were the heads of … , then this is what we would do. We'd …

Allow students a few minutes to look through the language in this unit before they discuss their ideas. Then divide the class into two groups. Each pair of students should explain their ideas to the bigger group, using second conditional structures. Other students can then comment on their ideas. For example:

If you did that, you'd go bankrupt within the year.

Review: Units 13–16

The exercises here can be used as a test. However, **4 Look back and check** and **8 What can you remember?** are better done as a discussion in pairs.

1 Tenses

Answers

1. 'll probably rain
2. were/was, I'd be
3. 'm doing, 'm just going to go
4. didn't live, 'd have
5. 'll pass, ask, ask, 'll probably fail
6. 'm dreading
7. 'll snow, does, does

2 Grammar review

Answers

1. I was thinking
2. it was going to rain, it doesn't look like it will
3. I'm really looking forward to
4. I doubt it'll be
5. It's bound to be
6. buying
7. to sack
8. I might, It depends

3 Prepositions

Answers

1. on	7. in
2. for	8. for
3. with	9. to
4. on	10. to, about
5. of	11. to
6. for	12. at

4 Look back and check

Answers

Answers will vary.

5 Verb collocations

Answers

1. i. 2. e. 3. a. 4. g. 5. b. 6. j. 7. c. 8. h.
9. d. 10. f.

6 Adjectives

Answers

1. rough
2. silly
3. sticky
4. damaged
5. dead
6. physical
7. long
8. saturated
9. pointless
10. aggressive

7 Questions and answers

Answers

1. d. 2. g. 3. j. 4. a. 5. b. 6. i. 7. c. 8. e.
9. f. 10. h.

8 What can you remember?

Answers

Answers will vary.

9 Common expressions

Answers

1. worth	6. left
2. tell	7. rather
3. trap	8. difference
4. short	9. what
5. burn	10. how

Answers for 11–13 will vary.

10 | Vocabulary quiz

Answers

1. Possible answers: the teacher bought drinks for his/her students, he/she sometimes doesn't show up for class, he/she makes fun of the students.

2. When you are on holiday.

3. By exercising more.

4. Possible answers: write the answers on your hand, look at someone else's paper for the answers, ask someone for the answers.

5. It is re-scheduled to happen on another day.

6. *A temple* is a place of worship for Hindus, Buddhists and Sikhs; *a mosque* is a place of worship for Muslims; *a church* is a place of worship for Christians.

7. By attracting all of the business for that market – maybe by taking over smaller, competing companies, by being given a state monopoly or by heavy/clever advertising.

8. Possible answers: try to get the teacher's attention, answer questions correctly all of the time, bring presents for the teacher.

9. Boiling hot.

10. Possible answer: You might feel disappointed or angry.

11. Businesses, stocks.

12. Answers will vary. You could mess up an exam by neglecting to answer some questions. You could mess up your driving test by hitting another car.

13. It was decided by insiders before the race who would win. One side was probably paid to lose.

14. Possible answers: Basketball and football.

15. It charges too much money.

16. He/she spends it on things he/she doesn't need – and then doesn't really use!

17. In the UK, *a degree* is more prestigious than *a diploma*. A degree is from a university and is given after three years' studying. It's nationally recognised and standardised. *A diploma* is usually in a vocational subject like nursing or teaching.

18. Possible answers: When you have to do something you don't want to do, or when you don't want to do something on your own.

19. Answers will vary. A hotel or resort might be *fully booked*. A concert or event could be *sold out*.

20. *I'll do it if I get the time* means that the person will try to do the task if he/she is not too busy. *I'd do it if I had the time* is hypothetical. It means the person does not have the time, and so (regrettably) will not do it.

Unit overview

General topic
Talking about family, friends and relationships.

Reading
Six different people explain what kind of person they are attracted to.

Language input

- Vocabulary for relatives: *mother-in-law, stepbrother, half brother*, etc.

- Adjectives to describe character: *out-going, fussy, big-headed*, etc.

- Expressions for describing when you met: *I've known her since I was a child. I met her when I was around thirty.* etc.

- Relationship verbs: *I'd fancied Anna for ages. I finally asked her out on a date.* etc.

- Pronunciation: linking: *No, I went with a friend of mine.*

- Expressions for talking about who you find attractive: *I want someone who is honest.* etc.

- Expressions for talking about what you're not looking for in a relationship: *I'd never go out with someone with a tatto*, etc.

- Expressions for guessing how old someone is: *He can't be older than eighteen. She must be in her late forties.* etc.

- Expressions with *used to* and *would*: *I used to make lots of mistakes when I first started learning Spanish. I'd get words mixed up and I'd speak bits of French by mistake and I'd forget things.*

Language strip

Use the language strip as a way to lead in to the unit. Ask students to quickly look through the list and find at least one expression that is either true or definitely not true for them. Explain that in this unit they will learn ways of talking about family, friends and relationships. Encourage them to choose some other expressions in the strip that look interesting and to find out more about them.

Use the language strip later on in this unit for a small group task. Ask students to find those expressions that could be used when talking about your family (e.g. *I'm one of four*) and those that could be used when talking about a relationship (e.g. *We've known each other for ages*). You might need to explain some of the following expressions:

- If you are *one of four*, you are one of four children in a family.

- If someone is your *half-brother* or *half-sister*, they have one parent in common with you.

- If you say something is *all history*, you are saying that it is past and is not important anymore. For example: *We used to fight terribly, but he's gone now, so it's all history.*

- If you describe two people as *an item*, you are saying that they are going out together. For example: *I've been seeing those two a lot together recently. Do you think they're an item?*

- If *you're not speaking to someone*, you have probably had a disagreement and don't want to talk to them any more. For example: *We're not speaking because of what she said about my Kevin.*

- If you *go for the strong, silent type*, you are attracted to quiet men who don't make a lot of fuss about things, but who are very supportive and caring.

Remind students to record any of the expressions that they like in their notebooks.

Lead in

As a lead in, brainstorm questions that have the word *family* in them. For example:
Do you get along with your family?
Do you come from a big family?
Do you want to settle down and start a family?

Write them on the board and have the class ask you. Then students can ask each other in small groups. You might want to explain the difference between *your immediate family* and *your extended family*.

Using vocabulary

1 Speaking

This exercise introduces some relationships that aren't often taught, so go over those that students may be unfamiliar with. You may need to explain that your *stepsister* is the daughter from a previous marriage of the man or woman your mother or father married. It might be easier to illustrate this relationship visually on the board using a family tree. You may need to explain that in English we don't differentiate between the two sides of a family. For example, the term for the mother of my wife and the mother of my husband is the same: *mother-in-law*. As a class, discuss how this may be different in students' own languages.

To do this exercise, have students go around the class asking questions. For example:
Have you got a … by any chance?
You haven't got a … have you?
Have you got a … , if you don't mind me asking?

Finish up by seeing who found the most people.

2 Adjectives

This exercise introduces some adjectives that can describe a person's character. Before students complete the exercise, tell them to find those adjectives that are positive and those that are negative. Encourage them to use a dictionary for those adjectives they are not sure of. The more positive ones are *independent, out-going, generous, liberal, easy-going, sporty* and *gorgeous*. The more negative ones are *strict, fussy, mean* and *big-headed*. *Quiet* and *religious* are either positive or negative depending on the point of view of the person using them. Students can then complete the sentences. Play the recording so that they can check their answers. Then have students ask each other the questions at the end.

Answers
1. strict
2. fussy…easy-going
3. independent, religious, generous
4. liberal
5. big-headed, mean
6. gorgeous, quiet
7. out-going, sporty

You may need to explain that *your gran* is your grandmother and that if you describe someone as *chatty*, they are friendly and like talking to people. Point out several other collocations here: *the exact opposite* and *very easy to get on with*.

3 Speaking

Explain that if *you don't know what someone sees in someone else*, you don't understand why the former is in a relationship with the latter, because the latter is not very appealing. Students can discuss this topic in small groups.

4 How did you meet?

This is a common question when talking about relationships. Although it is commonly used about romantic relationships, it is also used to talk about friends. Have students work individually through the two matching tasks and then check their answers with a partner, with one person reading 1–4 and the other giving the appropriate response a–d; students then switch over for 5–8. Have them explain why the verbs in some answers are in the present perfect (e.g. *I've known*

her since I was a child) and in others are in the past simple (*I met her when I was twenty-four*).

Answers
1. b. 2. d. 3. a. 4. c. 5. g. 6. f. 7. e. 8. h.

Before having students talk about their friends in small groups, tell them about one of your best or oldest friends. Explain how you met and what they are like. You may need to explain that *go out with* can either be about someone you are in a romantic relationship with, for example, *Are you two going out, then?* or about socialising, for example, *Do you fancy going out with us tonight?*

5 A pathetic story

The focus of this exercise is on some verbal expressions to describe a relationship. Students can work individually on the re-ordering task before checking their answers with a partner. Then they can discuss the questions at the end. Encourage students to record these expressions in their notebooks. Remind them that they could record them in a section about relationships as well as on a page where they are collecting expressions with *get* or phrasal verbs with *out*, etc. You may need to explain that if you *dump someone*, you decide to stop having a relationship with them.

Answers
The correct order is: 1. c. 2. e. 3. a. 4. d. 5. b.

Before moving on to the next exercise, you could have pairs of students close their books and try to recall the story from some verbs that you write on the board: *fancy, ask out, go out, met, see, get serious, leave, work out, get back together, get lost*

6 Pronunciation: linking

This exercise gives students more practice with linking within phrases. Help students see that in the two expressions at the start *my friend* is referring to a specific friend. The listener probably knows who you are talking about, perhaps because you only have one friend. *A friend of mine*, on the other hand, could be one of several friends you have from work. Play the recording all the way through so students can hear how the words are linked. Then play it again, pausing after each sentence so that students can repeat. Have pairs of students practise by alternately asking *Did you go on your own?* and saying the response. If possible, have them read the response to themselves, look up, and say it to their partner to help with the linking.

7 | Speaking

You might want to model this task for students before they do it themselves. For example:

A: *I went to that new club the other day.*
B: *Really? Did you go on your own?*
A: *No, I went with a few friends from work.*
B: *What was it like? Did you have a good time?*
A: *It was OK. I wasn't really into the music they were playing, though*

Encourage students to add a follow-up question and answer.

Reading

1 | Speaking

Focus students' attention on the photos of the people on page 122. Get them in pairs to talk about whether they find any of them attractive. Write some expressions on the board to help them:

I (don't) really go for …
I (don't) like the way she/he looks/dresses.
I don't find him/her all that attractive.
She/he's a bit too … for me.

You could also have students think about the kind of personality they think each person has. Teach the phrases *I bet* and *I reckon* to make guesses and encourage the use of some of the adjectives from **2 Adjectives** on page 120:

A: *I bet the man in the first picture on the left is very quiet.*
B: *I don't know. Look at that smile. I reckon he's rather out-going.*

2 | While you read (What's your type?)

Introduce the article and explain the task. Students can then read about the six people and share their reaction in pairs. Ask students what they think the title **What's your type?** means. Then play the recording of the article while students follow in the Coursebook. Encourage them to underline, ask about, or record any interesting expressions or collocations, particularly those they think they might use themselves. You may want to point out the following in any case:

I've changed my mind about …
I'm the wrong person to ask
she was everything I was looking for
I've lowered my standards

3 | Language focus

In this exercise, students are introduced to more ways to describe people, and also two patterns from the reading text. Get students to do the first task in pairs, and then decide if these descriptions are generally positive or negative.

> **Answers**
>
> Possible answers:
> a bit of an introvert: Alfonso
> fashion-conscious: Chiara
> unlucky in love: Thorsten/Alfonso
> desperate: Thorsten
> quite fussy: Chiara, Seon-Hee
> content: Lauren
> health-conscious: Rie
> less fussy than he used to be: Thorsten
> a bit strange: Seon-Hee
> fit: Rie

Have students complete the next task and then draw their attention to the patterns. Two of the three patterns contain a relative clause with *(someone) who*. The third *(someone) with* is an alternative to the relative clause *(someone) who has*. Students see that *'d (would)* and the 'past' tense express the unlikelihood of the person actually going out with a person like this. Have students record these patterns with their own personalised examples in their notebooks. Point out the collocation *strong political views*. Ask students if they know of any other nouns, apart from the obvious, that collocate with *strong (argument, marriage, accent)*.

> **Answers**
>
> 1. c. f. h. k.
> 2. a. d. g. l.
> 3. b. e. i. j.

4 | How old are they?

Ask students to complete either of the following with reference to age:

If I wasn't already in a relationship, I'd be looking for someone …

I'm looking for someone …

Listen to a few suggestions before talking about the fact that you would probably not mention a specific age. Then explain that in this exercise, students will see various expressions that talk about age in an unspecific way. Students can do the first task individually and then check in pairs.

Point out the two structures here that are used for guessing:

He/she must be …
He/she can't be …

Explain that we use *must* to say that we are quite sure something is true when we have evidence for it, and *can't* to say that we are quite sure something isn't true. Practise the pronunciation of the phrases, so that students can use them in the activities at the end of the exercise. Do these in small groups.

5 Speaking

Ask students to explain the difference between *in his forties* and *in the forties* before discussing the questions in small groups.

Write some expressions on the board to help them talk about these questions. For example:
I think life was much easier/harder in …
People had a lot more … in …
Music/clothes from the … are coming back into fashion.
These days, the fashion/music from the … looks/sounds …

Using grammar

1 Used to, would

This section explicitly focuses on *used to* and *would*; however, students will have seen many examples already in the Coursebook. The listening task gives students the opportunity to hear several more contextualised examples before they focus on the 'rules' in **2 Grammar study**.

Lead in by discussing the first question as a class. Talk a little about how you have changed yourself before asking students to do the same. Then introduce the listening task and explain what students have to do. Play the recording once and have students choose the right picture and talk about the differences. Then have them work on sentences 1–5. Play the recording again so that they can check their answers. You may need to explain that if you are *a bit of a ladies' man*, you enjoy spending time with women and want them to find you attractive. Play the recording one more time as students follow the tapescript on page 157.

2 Grammar study

Have students read the grammar explanations and ask about anything that they are not sure of. You may need to explain that *a state* refers to things that we don't see as actions. Ask students to tell you some verbs that are often used to describe a state rather than an action, for example, *be, own, live,* etc. Remind students to record complete examples of *used to*, including any time phrases in their notebooks. Point out that the negative is more commonly expressed as *never used to*.

3 Practice

Although this exercise practises expressions with *used to*, it reinforces verb + noun collocations as well.

When students have finished, model the pronunciation of *used to* and have them practise reading the sentences. Then have them memorise the second half of the sentences a–i and test each other, with one person reading the first part 1–9 and the other person completing the sentence without looking at the Coursebook.

4 Follow-up comments

Would has a similar meaning to *used to*. However, it often is used as a follow-up to *used to* and is only used for repeated actions, not states. Draw students' attention to the contraction in the examples. Once students have matched the follow-up comments, have them practise reading the statements in **3 Practice** and the follow-up comments together.

5 Free practice

Give students a true example about yourself first. For example:
When I was younger, I used to be really sporty. I'd go to the gym every other evening and I'd play football every weekend.

Have students go around talking to several people before getting the class back together to find out if there are any people who used to do the same sort of things.

6 Situations

It is common to keep conversations going by asking questions in response to what someone has said. This exercise practises this in the context of responding to someone explaining what they used to do. When checking answers, have students practise the intonation patterns of the questions. For the second task, you might want to do the first conversation as an example to show how the conversation can be extended. For example:

A: I used to live in Spain.
B: Oh, really? Whereabouts exactly?
A: I was in Madrid, the capital.
B: And why did you leave?
A: Well, I was there with my family. My dad worked for the embassy. We were there for about seven years until I was twelve and then we moved back home.
B: It must've been nice to grow up in another country.
A: Yeah, it was.

Then get students to practise these conversations in pairs.

Answers

Possible answers:
1. Whereabouts exactly? Why did you leave?
2. Were you any good? Why did you stop?
3. How many a day? When did you cut down?
4. What kind of thing? Poetry? Why did you stop?
5. Were you any good? Why did you stop?
6. What were you doing there? Why did you leave?

7 Speaking

Explain that if you *go off something*, you no longer like it. If you *go off the idea of doing something*, you no longer want to do it because it is no longer attractive to you. Tell students your own answers to some of the questions before having them discuss them in small groups. You may want to point out how *used to* is like a regular past tense verb in that in negatives and questions it is *use to*. However, the pronunciation is exactly the same as *used to*.

Follow-up

For a writing task, have students imagine that they are one of the people in the reading text on page 122 **What's your type?** Each person managed to find their ideal partner. However, several years has gone by, and while at first they were very happy, things have changed. They should write a letter explaining why they are going to leave their partner. Encourage the use of *used to* explain how the relationship was once good. For example:
You used to give me flowers. I loved the way you used to call me every day from work. I'd always look forward to the phone ringing because I knew it might be you. But now you hardly ever talk to me!

When students have finished, have them exchange letters with another person and then talk about what they have read.

18 Nationalities, festivals and languages

Unit overview

General topic
Talking about festivals, languages and stereotypes.

Reading
Four people describe famous festivals.

Language input

- Vocabulary for talking about festivals: *There's a big parade. There's a huge street party. It's become a bit too commercial.* etc.
- Relative clauses: *I didn't get that job I applied for. It's one of those things you cut your nails with. What do you call a person who can't stop drinking and is always drunk?*
- Vocabulary to talk about language: *mother tongue, a strong accent, minority languages,* etc.
- Expressions for disagreeing: *How can you say that? Come on! That's a bit of an exaggeration.* etc.
- Talking about stereotypes: *She's a typical small-town girl – really conservative! Oh, come on! Just because you don't come from the city, it doesn't mean you can't be open-minded.* etc.

Language strip

Use the language strip as a way to lead in to the unit. Ask students to quickly look through the list and find one expression that is connected with each of the following: nationality (*Scandinavians are usually blond, aren't they?*), festivals (e.g. *It's a big festival of the Arts*), and languages (e.g. *Are you bilingual, then?*). Explain that in this unit, they will learn other ways to talk about these areas. Encourage them to choose some other expressions that look interesting and to find out more about them.

Use the language strip later on in this unit for a small group task. Ask students to look at the expressions with *it* and discuss what this could be referring to. For example, *It's a big festival of the Arts* could be referring to the Edinburgh Festival. Students could also try to answer some of the questions (e.g. *How do you celebrate New Year in your country?*).

You might need to explain some of the following expressions:

- There is no such language as *Swiss*, so someone asking the question *Does anyone speak Swiss?* wouldn't know much about Switzerland! German, French and Italian are all widely spoken in Switzerland.
- *Scandinavians are usually blond, aren't they?* implies a stereotypical image of people from Scandinavia.

- If you say a place is *right on the border*, you are emphasising that it is almost exactly on the border. *Right* is often used for emphasis. For example: *It's right next to the bank. It's right in front of you.*
- *The Canaries* are a group of islands in the Atlantic and belong to Spain.
- If you describe a place as *cosmopolitan*, people from many different countries and cultures live there. For example: *New York is one of the most cosmopolitan places I've been to.*
- A *fiesta* is a big public celebration, especially a religious festival. They are very common in many Spanish-speaking countries. English has borrowed the word *fiesta*, so the English for *fiesta* is *fiesta*. English also uses the French word *fete* for a small outdoor celebration with games and stalls selling things like home-made cakes and jams.

Remind students to record any of the expressions that they like in their notebooks.

Lead in

You could use some of the questions in the language strip to lead in to the topic of festivals. Ask students if they have any big festivals of the Arts in their country or city, how they celebrate New Year and what some examples of old folk traditions in their country are. If you are from a different country from your students, talk about some of these things yourself.

Reading

1 Vocabulary

This exercise introduces some vocabulary to do with festivals. Point out the pictures A–H on page 126 and have students work in pairs matching them to the sentences 1–8. After checking their answers, have students go back and underline the collocations and transfer them to their notebooks. You should explain that *a bonfire* is a big fire lit as part of a celebration, or sometimes just to burn rubbish.

Answers							
1. h	2. d	3. a	4. f	5. g	6. b	7. c	8. e

2 Speaking

Get students in small groups to discuss these questions. Have them make guesses about all the pictures on page 126. Write some expressions on the board to help. For example:

It looks like it's in …
Isn't that the festival in … ?
I bet it's got something to do with …
It's probably in …

3 While you read (Four experiences)

Introduce the topic of the reading text task and explain. Point out the collocation *hold a festival*. Ask if students know some other events that we use with *hold* (e.g. *a meeting, a conference*). Have them read the text and then share their reactions with a partner. Write the following sentence starters on the board for them to use if necessary:

One thing I learned was that …
One thing I was surprised about was that …
I was surprised that …
I didn't realise that …
I always thought that …

Answers

Notting Hill Carnival is picture H.
The Glastonbury festival is picture F.
Fallas is picture C.
Hounen Matsuri is picture G.

---

4 Comprehension

Get students to discuss these questions in pairs. Encourage them to try to remember the answers without referring to the text. Then play the recording of the text as the class follow in the Coursebook, checking their answers. Here are some examples of questions you can ask as you go through the answers:

What expression could you use to say you do something every two days/weeks? (every other day/week)

What are some things you do out of habit?

What are the patron saints of some countries you know?

What kinds of thing do people celebrate in a festival marking the arrival of spring?

Answers

1. He goes every other year.
2. It's become too big.
3. A lot of people go there just to drink and take drugs.
4. Out of habit.
5. To commemorate the patron saint of the city.
6. A falla is a papier-mache model.
7. To celebrate the start of spring.

Have students go back through the reading text – you may want to play the recording again as they do this – finding any interesting expressions or collocations. You may want to point out the following:

broaden my mind
make friends
miles away
the festival runs (all through the beginning of March)

You may need to explain that if you say *there are literally thousands of people there*, you think that there are really thousands of people there. This is because we often exaggerate numbers and amounts. For example:
The stages seem to be miles away.
I've got millions of things to do.

Here is some information about the festivals not mentioned in the article.
Picture E is of the Songkran festival, which is held in Thailand from April 13 for the beginning of the traditional new year. People soak each other with water, symbolising the cleansing for a new year.
Picture A is of the Oktoberfest, which is a two-week festival in Munich, ending on the first Sunday of October. Large beer halls are erected and beer specially brewed for the occasion is served.
Picture B is the Berlin Love Parade, a huge annual street party in Berlin, Germany. It is famous for its techno music.

5 Speaking

Go over the questions before having students discuss them in groups. Explain that if something has become *too commercial*, you think that the making of money has become the most important thing. We sometimes describe films or music as *commercial* when we think they are released to a wide audience and expect high sales numbers. You might also give some examples of things that might be embarrassing for young people in your country. In the UK, young people might be embarrassed by traditional folk dancing – morris dancing.

6 Vocabulary focus

This exercise helps students distinguish between the words *commemorate* and *celebrate*. Have students complete the two definitions and then do the matching exercise. Then have them underline the complete expressions in the sentences here and transfer them to their notebooks. Point out the collocations *hold a special ceremony* and *a fancy restaurant*. Explain that *a ceremony* is a special event that is characterised by more or less fixed, traditional words and actions, for example, *a wedding ceremony, an award ceremony, the opening ceremony*. It is usually formal. If something is *fancy* it is more expensive or of a higher quality than normal, for example, *a fancy car, a fancy house*.

Answers

a. celebrate, celebrate
b. commemorate

1. d.   2. a.   3. f.   4. e.   5. c.   6. b.

Before students talk about the questions at the end in small groups, tell them about some public holidays or local festivals you know. For the last question, you could use this example:

A friend of mine passed her driving test this year. Do you know how many times she had taken it? Eight. She was beginning to feel like she'd never pass. Anyway, her boyfriend was so impressed. Guess what he did to celebrate? He only went out and bought her a brand new car!

Using grammar

1 Relative clauses

In this exercise, students focus on relative clauses that can omit the relative pronoun *that*. *That* generally replaces the relative pronouns *who(m)* or *which* when the relative clause is defining i.e., it gives information that defines the noun. For example:
Where's the book *that/which* I lent you?

That can be omitted when it acts as an object in the relative clause, but can't be omitted when it is the subject. For example:

Where's the book (that) I lent you? (that = object)

I need something that can go more than 60 miles per hour! (that = subject)

One easy way to think about this is that if *that* is followed by a pronoun, it can be left out; if *that* is followed by a verb, it has to stay. Ask students to look at the example and to read the explanation. Answer any questions they may have before doing the matching exercise. You may want to remind students of the patterns they met in the previous unit:
I want someone who …
I'd never go out with someone who …

In these cases *that* could replace *who*, but can't be omitted because it acts as the subject of the relative clause.

Answers							
1. e.	2. a.	3. g.	4. c.	5. d.	6. b.	7. f.	8. h.

Draw students' attention to the position of the prepositions in a, b, d, e, g and h. For the last task, the follow-up exercise, go around the class and check students' answers before asking some people to tell the class a few of their answers.

Answers

Possible answers:

2. Hey, there's that girl you used to go out with.
3. You should try that restaurant our teacher mentioned.
4. I couldn't do that homework you told me about.

---

5. Hey, I went and saw that film you suggested.
6. Do you sell those things you clean your ears out with?
7. We had a good holiday, but the car we rented was far too big.
8. Have you seen those new mobile phones they've started selling?

Finally, ask a few questions about some of the other language here:
What kinds of places have canteens? (work places, schools)

What else can you apply for, apart from a job? (a grant, a leave of absence)

Can you think of some other reasons why you might be really disappointed?

2 Practice

Do an example with the class to give them the idea of how to do this. Describe an object like a watering can, for example, and have students draw it.
It's one of those things you water plants with. It's got a handle and a thing the water comes out of.

Remind students of the words *thing* and *stuff*, which they might find useful in their descriptions. You could also give them this pattern:
It's one of those things you use to …

Finish up by having students ask you about any of the things they couldn't find the name of in the last task.

3 Questions with relative clauses

The explanation at the start of this exercise reinforces the fact that relative clauses describe nouns. Go over the explanation with students and answer any questions they may have. Then do the first question as an example. You could either have students work on this in pairs or individually.

Answers

1. What are the (two) people you share a flat with like?
2. What was that hotel you stayed in in Paris like?
3. What was that club you went to on Friday like?
4. What are the other people you work with like?
5. What was that restaurant you went to for your birthday like?
6. What was that English course you did in Australia like?
7. What did you do in that class I missed last week?
8. What was that school you studied at in Sydney called?
9. Did you get that job you applied for?

For the second task, act out the first conversation with a student as an example:

A: *What are the people you live with like?*
B: *They're really friendly. Really nice.*
A: *You're lucky. The people I live with are awful.*
B: *Why do you say that?*
A: *They're not very friendly at all. They hardly ever speak to me.*

4 | Defining people

Here students see another example of a relative clause, this time with the relative pronoun *who*. It's possible to use *that* in place of *who* in these examples, but *a person who* tends to be more common. Ask students if they notice that in the examples here, *who* acts as the subject of the relative clause. Point out the expression *the 'real' Japan* in the explanation. Explain that this means the traditional, rural Japan, not the modern, westernised, urban Japan. Ask what tourists who think like this would believe the 'real' country is in the student's country. Ask if this perception of their country is correct.

Students can work on the dictionary task in pairs. Before you check their answers, you could write this pattern on the board to show how we can use a similar relative clause structure for giving a definition:

A … is someone who …

Then have students write the definitions in their notebooks. Point out the collocation *perform operations*. Give students some more examples of nouns that collocate with *perform* (e.g. *a ceremony, a trick, miracles*).

Answers

1. an alcoholic   2. a workaholic   3. an undertaker
4. a surgeon   5. a journalist   6. a juggler

Use the pictures of people on page 129 to help students generate some ideas for the second task, but encourage them to think of other things as well. It may help them to imagine if they were doing it in their own language.

Listening

1 | Speaking

This exercise shifts the topic away from festivals to language and stereotypes. Students can use their dictionaries for the first task. When checking their answers, write an example of how some of the terms can be used:

Where's your accent from?
They speak in a strong dialect up in the north.
I didn't know their mother tongue was French.
English is the lingua franca of international business.
'Keep shtum' is a slang term meaning 'keep quiet'.
I think there's too much swearing on TV these days.
She's virtually bilingual in French and English.

Answers

1. *An accent* is the way you pronounce the language, while *a dialect* is a form of the language that is spoken in a particular area or by a particular group of people.

2. *Your mother tongue* is the language you learn from your parents, while *a lingua franca* is a language used to communicate between people who don't speak each other's mother tongues.

3. *Slang* is very informal language that can be particular to a certain time or group of people, while *swearing* is the use of rude or offensive language.

4. If you are *bilingual,* you grew up learning two languages and can speak both of them equally well, while if you can speak *a foreign language,* you may have just learned it later in life and you probably don't speak it as well as your mother tongue.

5. If you have *a slight accent,* your pronunciation is a little different from what is considered standard, while if you have *a strong accent,* there is a big difference.

Before having students discuss the questions in the second task, make sure they understand the expressions *a minority language* and *have a higher status*.

Reading

2 | Reading

Focus attention on the title (**English teacher sacked for speaking English!**) and have students predict what the article is about. Then ask students to read the text and share their reactions in pairs. Ask them if the title was really accurate. At this point, you might want to tell your students a little about the Welsh language. Although England took control of Wales in the thirteenth century, Wales was better able to preserve its original language and culture than other areas of the British Isles. Its language is still widely used and about 25% of people are bilingual in Welsh and English. There is a strong movement to encourage the use of Welsh.

3 | Radio interview

Explain the task and play the recording of the interview. Then have students compare notes in pairs before playing the recording again so they can check their answers. Ask students if this changed their mind about Gareth Davies and his situation at all.

Answers

Arguments for: Christine says that Welsh is dying out. When the language dies, you also lose the culture and traditions of the country. Languages need to be protected.

Arguments against: Gareth says you can't make people learn languages. People have a right to speak their language of choice.

4 | Disagreeing

This exercise introduces some expressions for disagreeing. Have students work on the first task alone and then compare answers in pairs. Play the recording so they can check.

Explain a few of the expressions.

- *Come on!* is often used when we think that what someone has said is ridiculous. For example:
  A: *It's freezing outside.*

  B: *Oh, come on! It's not that bad.*

- If you make *an exaggeration*, you make something sound greater, more important, more, etc. Than it really is. For example:
  A: *So, there were millions of people on march, then?*

  B: *Well, OK that's a bit of an exaggeration.*

- If you say *let's just agree to disagree*, you are indicating that you no longer want to argue because it is clear that both sides are not going to change their position.

Answers

1. Come on! That's a bit of an exaggeration!
2. So what you're saying is
3. Do you honestly believe that?
4. How can you say that?
5. Listen, we're obviously never going to agree
6. Let's just agree to disagree

Play the recording again, pausing after each gap to practise the intonation. Then have pairs of students read the conversations. Encourage them to use these expressions in the pair work task.

5 | Speaking

This exercise gives students an opportunity to use some of the expressions from **4 Disagreeing**. Review some of the other language from previous units that might be useful here too. For example:
Personally, I think …
Definitely!
That's the way I see it too.
I know (what you mean).

Go around the class, monitoring students as they discuss these issues and collect examples of language difficulties to go over later. Finish up by having groups briefly report back on what they talked about. To follow up this activity, have pairs of students choose one of the questions and write a dialogue like the radio interview between two people with opposing views.

6 | Stereotypes and reality

Lead in by focusing students' attention on the picture and ask which country is being shown and how they knew. Then ask students to think of what British people are typically like. Listen to their answers and explain that when we have a general image of a group of people like this, we often call it a stereotype. Explain that if someone fits a stereotype, the general image is true about that person. You might also want to give some other collocations. For example:
reinforce a stereotype
a popular stereotype

This exercise revises some character adjectives and introduces some more character adjectives as well. Students can use their dictionaries for those they are unsure of. You may need to explain the following:

- If you describe someone as *arrogant*, you don't like the way they act because they think they are better than other people

- If you describe someone as *snobbish*, you don't like the way they act because they think they are better than other people, perhaps because they have a higher social status or more money.

Play the recording so students can check their answers. Then play it again so students can follow the intonation patterns and respond chorally. They can then practise with a partner.

Answers

1. generous 2. quiet 3. out-going 4. open-minded
5. nice 6. distant 7. dull 8. Two-faced

Point out the expressions that are common responses to overgeneralisations like:
Every … I've ever met was …
I've got a really good friend who's … and she/he's …
That's such a stereotype!
Just because you …it doesn't mean you …

Write these responses on the board so students can refer to them when they have their own conversations about other stereotypes. You may want to talk about how numbers 1, 2, 3, 5 and 6 are about stereotypes English people have, and that number 8 features a stereotype English people have about themselves.

Follow-up

Have students write a description of a festival from their own country or community, or, in a monolingual class, ask them to find out about a festival from another country. They should explain what the festival commemorates or celebrates, when it is held, what happens, whether people dress up, etc. They should also try to use relative clauses to define any special equipment or any special roles people have. When students have finished, ask them to exchange papers with a partner. They should read their partner's description and then talk about what they read.

Unit overview

General topic
Crimes and punishment; Celebrity criminals.

Reading
The cases of nine celebrity criminals.

Language input

- Crimes and law vocabulary: *found guilty, get six months, tax evasion, speeding*, etc.

- Expressions for reacting to criminal cases: *He got off lightly. He should've got life for that.* etc.

- Expressions for saying an approximate number: *around $4.5 million, about $300 million, over 90 miles an hour, almost $150,000.*

- Vocabulary associated with crimes: *she'd been stabbed, this kid went on the rampage, they held a gun to my head*, etc.

- Third conditional expressions: *I'm sure I would've done better if I'd dressed a bit more smartly for the interview. If I'd known, I wouldn't have bothered.* etc.

Language strip

Use the language strip as a way to lead in to the unit. Ask students to quickly look through the list. Explain that in this unit they will learn how to talk about crimes and punishments. Encourage them to choose expressions in the language strip that look interesting and to find out more about them.

Use the language strip later on in this unit for a small group task. Ask students to find those expressions that refer to a trial (e.g. *The jury found her not guilty*) and those that just refer to a crime (e.g. *He mugged an old lady in the park*). Then ask students to choose a couple of the expressions containing *he, she* or *they*. They should then discuss what the story behind the expression might be. For example, students could use *The jury found her not guilty* to speculate what 'she' was on trial for, why she was found not guilty, whether she really committed the crime or not, etc. You might need to explain some of the following expressions:

- If *someone got life*, they received a life sentence for a crime. This means that they will be in prison for quite a long time, usually at least twenty years. It does not necessarily mean they will be there for the rest of their life, though.

- If you say *someone got what they deserved*, you think that the bad thing that has happened to them (e.g. receiving a harsh sentence) is justified because of

what they originally did. For example: *I think he got what he deserved. If you bring a weapon to school, you should be expelled right away.*

- If *someone mugs someone*, they attack a person in a public place in order to steal their money or valuables. For example: *Did you hear he was mugged on his way home last night?*

- If *someone got away with millions*, they managed to steal millions of pounds, dollars, etc. and escape without being caught. For example: *Did you hear about that shop that was held up last week? Apparently, they got away with over a thousand pounds.*

- If the police *drop the charges against someone*, they no longer want to continue pursuing the legal process against someone they originally accused of doing something illegal. For example: *I think they should drop the charges against him. No jury is going to find him guilty.*

- If women *go topless*, they don't wear anything to cover their breasts. Some collocations for *topless* include *a topless bar* and *sunbathe topless*.

- If you refer to someone as *a dealer*, you are usually implying that they are a drug dealer. The word *dealing* is also used to refer to drug dealing. For example: *You can go to jail if you're caught dealing.*

- If you think that *they should lock someone up and throw away the key*, you think that the person should go to prison for the rest of their life. For example: *When they catch the person who mugged that old lady, they should lock him up and throw away the key.*

- *Three strikes and you're out* refers to the policy whereby if you are found guilty of certain crimes for the third time, you are sent to prison. It is also used for other situations to mean if you do something wrong three times, you will no longer be able to be somewhere or do something. For example: *We have a three strikes and you're out policy. If you're late three times, you're expelled.*

- If *someone is over the limit*, they have had more alcohol than is legally allowed while driving a car. For example: *She was three times over the limit. No wonder she lost her licence.*

Remind students to record any of the expressions that they like in their notebooks.

Lead in

One way to lead in is to have students brainstorm a list of crimes. Divide the class up into small groups and give them five minutes to think of the names of as many crimes as they can and write them down. Go around the class and monitor and help when necessary. Then put the following patterns on the board:

… is a serious problem in my/this country.
… is unheard of in my/this country.
… is quite common in my/this country.

Students can then use these patterns to talk about the crimes they have listed. When they have finished, you can go on to the first exercise and students can compare their list with the one in the book.

Reading

1 Speaking

This exercise introduces vocabulary associated with the legal process and the names of different crimes. You could start off by asking students to close their Coursebooks and read the introduction yourself. Encourage students to ask you any questions and then put these words up on the board: *crime, court, guilty, judge, fine, six months, life*. Ask them, in pairs, to recall the phrases you used these words in. Then let them read the introduction in the Coursebook to see if they were right.

Go through the list of crimes with students to make sure they understand them. You might want to contrast *possession of drugs* with *dealing in drugs*. Explain that *burglary* usually refers to breaking into private homes and stealing things. You should also explain that *murder* is the crime of killing someone intentionally, while *manslaughter* the crime of killing someone, but without the intent of doing so. Point out that all of these crimes can be used with *(found) guilty of …* . However, not all of them can be used with *commit*.

You could either discuss the sentences for the list of crimes as a class or in small groups. In either case write the pattern on the board:
You'd probably get … for … .

Students may not know exactly what sentences might be received for each crime, so you could encourage them to use expressions like:
You'd definitely go to prison.
You'd probably just get a fine.

Depending on where your students are from, you could also teach them *get the death penalty*. If they want to record this crime vocabulary in their notebooks, encourage them to include an example of how the word(s) are used in this exercise. For example:
If you're found guilty of possession of drugs, you'd just get a fine.

Remind them to include an appropriate translation too.

Focus students' attention on the photos and then get them in pairs to talk about what kind of crime they think the people committed. Write some language on the board to help. For example:
I think I read somewhere that he was found guilty of …
Wasn't he the one who … ?

2 While you read (Rich and Famous or Rich and Dangerous?)

Explain the task to your students and divide them into two groups. Remind them that they should initially just read to find out what the people in the photos did. After students have finished reading, get them into pairs so that they can share what they found out. Write some example questions on the board to get them started:
What did he do?
Was he found guilty?
What did he get?

You could then have students read the half of the text that they haven't read yet. Finally, play the recording as students follow along in the Coursebook, underlining any interesting collocations and expressions. You might want to point out the following, which are connected to the topic of the unit:
he was accused of
clear evidence
he was sentenced to six years in prison
he was taken to court
he took the paper to court
if it had gone to court
the truth came out eventually
he was charged with smuggling
he paid a one hundred and forty thousand dollar fine

You might also want to have students find all the *get* expressions in the text:
the jury got it wrong
he was lucky to get away with it
he got out just three years later for good behaviour
Archer's story-telling had got a bit out of control
he could've got seven years and a $2,000 fine

3 Common expressions

In this exercise, students are introduced to several expressions for giving a reaction to a crime or trial. You might want to start off by just asking them what they think about one of the celebrities. Listen to their ideas and then focus their attention on the expressions. Explain that if you think *someone got off lightly*, you think they only received a very small punishment, but that if you think *the sentence was a bit harsh*, you think it was too severe. Point out that *There's one law for the rich and another one for the poor* is a fairly fixed expression. Ask students if they can think of any other situations they know that this expression can be applied to. Then get them in pairs to react to the different cases.

4 Speaking

Use these questions for a small group discussion. You might want to start off by telling the students of any other cases that you know of, especially any where the person was eventually found innocent. Encourage them to ask you questions and react using any of the expressions in **3 Common expressions**. Go around monitoring and collecting examples of language difficulties to go over when students have finished.

5 Numbers

To illustrate how we are frequently not specific in talking about numbers, ask a few students some questions like *How long does it take you to get to school in the morning?* The interaction could go something like this:

A: *How long does it take you to get to school in the morning?*
B: *One hour.*
A: *You mean exactly one hour?*
B: *No, about one hour.*
A: *You're lucky, that's quite fast. It usually takes me over two hours.*

Then, go over the examples. Check that students know the meanings of the words in the box, and then get them in pairs to talk about the numbers in 1–11. Note that in several of the examples there could be more than one answer. Play the recording so students can compare their answers. Stop after each one to ask if anyone had a different answer. Play the recording again to let students listen to the pauses and intonation. Then play it one more time, pausing after item so that students can repeat chorally. Finally, have groups of two or more students practise saying the expressions.

> **Answers**
>
> 1. about/almost/around one hundred and fifty kilometres an hour
> 2. about/over/around half an hour late
> 3. about/almost/around three hundred and twenty-five
> 4. about/almost/around a thousand
> 5. about/around five hundred
> 6. about/almost/around five thousand
> 7. about/around one hundred thousand
> 8. about/around three and a half million
> 9. about/almost/around ten million
> 10. about/around/over seventy-eight million
> 11. about/almost/around two hundred million

6 Free practice

Students can ask and answer these questions in pairs. You could also write some expressions on the board to help. For example:
It must be about/almost/around/over …
I'm sure it can't be more than …
At a rough guess I'd say …

Finish up as a class by listening to what students have come up with. React to their ideas with expressions like:
That's quite harsh/not much/a bit high.
Really? That much? Are you sure about that?

Encourage students to react using these expressions as well.

> **Answers**
>
> Answers will of course vary, but if the speed limit on the motorway is 110 kilometres per hour, the equivalent will be about seventy miles per hour. In 2001 the population of China was estimated at 1,273,111,300 – almost one point three billion!

Using vocabulary

1 Basic crime vocabulary

Students can work through this exercise in pairs, using their dictionaries when necessary. When they have finished, go through the answers and ask follow-up questions on some of the vocabulary:
What kind of weapon is used for stabbing? (a knife, a screwdriver, anything sharp)
What else can you raid? (a bank, a post office, any kind of public building. You can also raid the fridge!)
What do you think the difference is between a massacre and a killing? (A massacre usually involves the killing of a lot of people. The word also emphasises that the killing was done in a violent or cruel way.)
Why do you think 'go on the rampage with a gun' was used instead of 'go around with a gun'? ('Go on the rampage' emphasises that the shooting was violent, and caused a lot of destruction or death.)
What else could someone have snatched? (a handbag, a laptop, a baby)
What else could you have come home to find? (the door wide open, the back window smashed)
What's the difference between 'a serial killer' and 'a killer'? (A serial killer kills several people, one after the other on different occasions. Often the victims are killed in a similar way. A killer is someone who kills.)

You could also ask students what kind of sentence a person would get for each crime. Point out the use of *apparently* in several of the conversations. Explain that this is often used when we are telling someone about something that we've heard about on the news or from a friend.

Answers

1.	a. murder	b. dead	c. stabbed
2.	a. robbery	b. raided	c. got away with
3.	a. massacre	b. rampage	c. killed
4.	a. snatched	b. came up to him	c. ran off
5.	a. burgled	b. kicked in	c. stolen
6.	a. serial killer	b. papers	c. killed

Model one of the conversations with a student to show how it could be extended before having them practise in pairs:

A: *Did you hear about that murder yesterday?*

B: *No, what happened?*

A: *They found this woman dead just near where I live. Apparently, she'd been stabbed six times.*

B: *That's terrible! Where did they find her? Was she in her flat?*

A: *No, they found her in the back of a van. Apparently it'd been parked there for a couple of days.*

2 Free practice

This exercise extends **1 Basic crime vocabulary** by changing some of the vocabulary. Point out the expression *five million in cash*. Do the first one as an example with the whole class. Encourage students to use a follow-up comment. For example:

A: *Did you hear about that murder yesterday?*

B: *No, what happened?*

A: *They found this old man dead in his house. Apparently, he'd been beaten to death.*

B: *That's terrible! I hope they catch the person who did it*

When students have finished, have them repeat the task with another student. Then get the them to walk around the class, talking about any recent crimes they've heard about.

3 Before you listen

Go through the sentences asking students to identify the corresponding pictures on page 135. Explain the expression *at knife-point* and mention we can also say *at gun-point*. You might want to point out that we use *go* with *shoplifting*. You could ask what other *-ing* words collocate with *go* – *go shopping, fishing, skiing, jogging, drinking*, etc. Ask students what they think should happen if children are caught shoplifting, who usually catches them (store detectives, security guards, etc.), and what powers they have. Then have them discuss the question at the end of the exercise either as a class or in small groups.

Answers

1. C   2. D   3. A   4. F   5. B   6. E

---

4 Four crimes

Explain the task and play the recording. Students can then compare their answers in pairs. Elicit the expressions connected to each one and put them on the board. Play the recording again as the class follow the tapescript on page 158. Then they can complete the correction task in pairs.

Answers

Person 1: A
Person 2: F
Person 3: D
Person 4: E

Person 3 made the following language mistakes:
I want to report that I was stolen my mobile phone.
I was walking by sea when two boys ran and one of boys take it.
I just do a one-day travel here … from Brighton.
Oh, you're only here on a day-trip.

The victim might have expressed himself correctly as follows:
I want to report that my mobile phone was/has been stolen.
I was walking by the sea when two boys came running/ran past me and one of them snatched it.
I am here on a day-trip from Brighton.

---

5 Vocabulary

This exercise reinforces some of the expressions from **4 Four crimes**. Let students work alone initially, and then have them compare their answers in pairs. Go through the answers yourself, asking further questions. For example:

Someone can hold a gun to your head, but where would they hold a knife to? (your throat)

What would you have to have done if your house keys were stolen? (have the locks changed)

How about if the door of your flat was kicked in? (have it replaced)

Why might someone leave their keys at home? (they were in a hurry, the keys were in a different jacket)

If you saw someone shoplifting, would you tell the police? Why/why not?

Then you can have pairs of students test each other. One person reads the sentence, saying 'blank' instead of the gapped word. Their partner, with their Coursebook closed, repeats the sentence, but includes the missing verb. Pairs of students can then work on the correction task before you play the recording so they can check their answers.

Answers

1. held   2. smashed   3. leave   4. got away with
5. report   6. snatched   7. let   8. cancelled

The differences between 1–8 and the conversations in the recording are:

1. They held a knife to the throat, not a gun to the head.

2. The back window had been smashed, not the car windscreen.

3. I left my keys in my car, not at home.

4. They got away with my handbag (and keys and home address), not my suitcase. It was on the back seat, not the boot.

5. He wanted to report he'd had his mobile phone snatched, not his bag.

6. He was walking along by the sea when he had his phone snatched by two boys, not by a man.

7. They let the security guards know, not the police.

8. The speaker hasn't actually cancelled the cards yet. In number 8, it says they cancelled the cards straightaway.

Using grammar

1 Third conditionals

In this unit, students focus on the structure often called the third conditional. You might want to review the first and second conditional structures before having them start this exercise. Write up some gapped examples from previous units:
… give you a hand if you …
A: Do you think they'll win?
B: If they … first,… have a chance.
If I … the money, … love to come, but I really can't afford it.
If it … mine, … lend it to you, but as he's not here I can't ask him.

Ask students if they remember the missing words. Ask what the time frame is and whether the speaker thinks the condition is possible or hypothetical. Then ask students to read the explanation and the examples of the third conditional. Answer any questions they have, and remind them that this structure talks about a hypothetical situation in the past.

2 Practice

Get students to do the matching task individually and then compare answers with a partner. Check the answers as a class, pointing out collocations and expressions as you go through them. For example:
my flat got broken into
burglar alarm

pleaded guilty
prove he was innocent
we missed the flight
I didn't get that job
dressed a bit more smartly
have a few more days there
halfway through the first half

Ask further questions where appropriate. For example:
Do you think a burglar alarm makes any difference?
What should he have worn at the interview?

Write the following two patterns on the board and encourage students to transfer some of the examples to their notebooks.
It wouldn't have happened if …
I'm sure I/we would've done if …

Answers

1. a.   2. e.   3. c.   4. b.   5. h.   6. g.   7. f.   8. d.

For the follow-up task, students focus on what actually happened, and so the hypothetical nature of the third conditional is reinforced. Go around monitoring students as they write their alternative *if-* clauses. Elicit a couple of suggestions for each question and write them on the board.

Answers

Possible answers:

2. It wouldn't have happened if I'd bolted the back door.

3. It wouldn't have happened if he'd told them where the money was hidden.

4. It wouldn't have happened if you'd got up at five like me.

5. I'm sure I would've done if I hadn't made that joke about his wife.

6. I guess you would've done if it'd been open.

7. I'm sure I would've done if I'd actually revised.

8. I'm sure we would've done if our goalkeeper hadn't been sent off.

---

3 Free practice

Give students an example yourself before they work on their own sentences:
I can't believe I overslept this morning. It wouldn't have happened if I'd stayed in and had an early night last night like I'd intended to.

They can then work on the next task in pairs. The answers are fairly predictable and include some common phrases: *if I hadn't been so busy, it would've been nicer if … , I wouldn't have asked, if I'd known.*

You could also ask students to think of variations here too like *I wouldn't have asked if I'd known her boyfriend was serving behind the bar.*

4 | Pronunciation: third conditionals

The examples here contain contractions that can be difficult for some students. Play the recording once all the way through. Ask students to listen to the intonation pattern. Then play it again. This time, ask them to mark the stressed words. Then play it a third time, pausing after sentence so that they repeat. Follow up by discussing as a class what students think each sentence could be referring to. Here are some ideas: Number 1 could mean *I asked someone about her boyfriend, only to find out he'd just left her for another woman!* Number 2 could mean *I made the effort to go to see a movie, but regret it now because it wasn't very good.* Number 3 could mean *I wore the same clothes as someone else to a party – and they looked better in them than I did!* Number 4 could mean *Someone has only just told me about their birthday party last Friday.* Number 5 could mean *I asked your parents about their jobs, only for you to now tell me they've both been made redundant recently.* Number 6 could mean *I saw a UFO or something else amazing.* Number 7 could mean *I had a great teacher at secondary school who inspired me.* Number 8 could mean *Somebody saved my life.* Number 9 could mean *I did lots of homework last weekend because I thought it was compulsory – now I find out it was optional!* Finally, number 10 could mean *I didn't do my homework – not because I'm lazy, but because it was optional, not compulsory.* Explain the expression *see it with my own eyes.* This is used to emphasise that something difficult to believe actually happened because you saw it. For example:
A: *You know she drives a Ferrari, don't you?*
B: *You're kidding!*
A: *No, I saw it with my own eyes. It's parked round the back.*

For the next task, remind students of the situation with Nick and Janet. Instead of reading the letter, students could listen to you read it aloud and then write a few third conditional sentences in pairs. Then they could use these for the basis of the role play. Have them write the dialogue and practise it a few times. Then get them to get together with another group and act it their dialogues to each other.

5 | Finally

Give information about any of the crimes students are not sure of and then get them to think for a few moments. Get them in pairs to briefly discuss their ideas for about five minutes before getting them in bigger groups of five or six to continue the discussion. Finish up by discussing as a class. You might want to add or substitute other crimes as you see fit.

- The Dunblane Massacre occurred in 1996 in a children's school in a small town in Scotland. A former caretaker burst into a class and shot twenty-eight five- and six-year-old children. Fifteen of the children and their teacher were killed. The man then killed himself.
- The Columbine High School shootings occurred in Colorado in the US in 1999. Two teenage students went into their high school and shot and killed twelve students and a teacher. They then killed themselves.
- Harold Shipman was a doctor in England. For over twenty years he murdered his patients by giving them lethal drug injections. It has been estimated that he killed up to 300 people. He's Britain worst serial killer.
- The Bali bombing occurred on 12th October 2002 on the island of Bali. Two packed clubs were destroyed by bombs. Over 200 people were killed. Some of the bombers got the death penalty. They were religious extremists.

Follow-up

Tell the class a few lateral thinking stories. Many of them are connected with crimes in one way or another. There are several ways to exploit them. You could just tell the class the basic puzzle and get them to ask you yes/no questions until they figure out the answer, or you could flesh out the story, adding little clues here and there, and use it for listening practice. Then students try to work out the solution in groups. You can find many of these stories on the Internet. Here is an example:
At 2:00 pm the burglar alarm went off at Vincent Pond's house. The police arrived. They found a broken window. Everything was thrown around. The air-conditioning was on. They discovered Vincent upstairs. He had been strangled. They phoned his wife, Patricia. She was playing golf. She said she had left home at 12:30. A witness confirmed that she had seen Patricia at the golf club at 1:15. At first, the police suspected a burglar, but three days later, Patricia remarried. The chief investigator is sure Patricia murdered Vincent before 12:30 and somehow got the burglar alarm to go off. There were no animals in the house, no electrical devices were used and Patricia acted alone. How did she do it?
(Answer: She put a tray on the edge of the kitchen table. On one side was a big bag of ice and on the other a saucepan. When the ice eventually melted, the pan fell on the floor setting off the motion sensor and activating the alarm.)

Unit overview

General topic

Health problems, advice and doctors.

Dialogue

David and Ken talk about recent visits to the doctor's.

Language input

- Verb collocations for health problems: *I've got an awful cold. I've cut my finger. I feel a bit sick.* etc.

- Giving advice: *Maybe you should take some aspirin or something.* etc.

- More health-related expressions: *allergic to, have a check-up, wear contact lenses,* etc.

- Reporting health advice: *He just told me to go home and take it easy. She gave me some painkillers for it.* etc.

- Differences between *should* and *have to/have got to* for giving advice: *You should try to lose a bit of weight. You have to register with the surgery first.*

- Expressions with *should* for making suggestions and talking about what we expect to happen: *You should try that new Italian place. It should be open by the end of next week.* etc.

- Pronunciation: sentence stress:
  A: *This is going to cost us a fortune.*
  B: *No. It shouldn't be that expensive.*

Language strip

Use the language strip as a way to lead in to the unit. Ask students to look quickly through the list to find any expressions that are true for them or that they could answer in the affirmative. Explain that in this unit they will learn ways of talking about health and giving advice. Encourage them to choose some other expressions in the strip that look interesting and to find out more about them.

Use the language strip later on in this unit for a small group task. Ask students to find those expressions that describe a problem (e.g. *I've had a really bad cold*) and those that give advice or make a suggestion (e.g. *Have you tried Chinese medicine?*). Then ask students to think of an answer for those expressions that are questions (e.g. *How are you?*).

You might need to explain some of the following expressions:

- *Homeopathy* is a way of treating illnesses by giving small amounts of a substance that in large amountswould cause the same illness.

- You might ask *How did you do it?* if someone said that they have hurt part of their body. For example:
  A: *I've done something strange to my back.*
  B: *How did you do it?*
  A: *I think it was when I was carrying that big box of books upstairs.*

- If you say that *someone could do with something*, you think that it would be good for them to have it or do it. For example: *You look as if you could do with a nice cup of tea.*

- If *you sprain your ankle or wrist*, you hurt it by twisting it. For example: *I hope it's just a sprained ankle.*

- If you're *feeling a bit run-down*, you're very tired and a little bit ill – usually because you've been working too much recently.

Remind students to record any of the expressions that they like in their notebooks.

Lead in

You could lead in immediately by focusing on the pictures and asking students what health problems they can see. Ask if anyone can remember when they last had one of them. Ask if anyone has never had, for example, a toothache. Then you can do **1 Collocations**.

Using vocabulary

1 Collocations

Explain the task and have students work individually and then compare their answers in pairs. You may need to explain the following:

- If *you have a stiff neck*, you have difficulty moving your neck because the muscles are painful.

- If *you are hung-over*, you feel ill in the morning after a night of drinking.

- If *you've got hay fever*, you are allergic to pollen.

As you go through the answers, point out the adjectives and modifiers: *an awful cold, a really stiff neck, a bit hung-over,* etc. Also draw students' attention to the vague expressions: *for some reason, I've done something strange* and *somehow.*

Answers		
1. got	7. got	13. got
2. got	8. feel	14. done
3. cut	9. got	15. sprained
4. sprained	10. feel	16. cut.
5. got	11. got	
6. done	12. got	

Review these collocations by having pairs of students test each other. One person can read sentences 1–8, saying 'blank' instead of the gapped word. Their partner, without looking at the Coursebook, responds by repeating the whole sentence with the missing verb. Students can then switch roles for 9–16.

For the next task, ask students what they would do if they had an awful cold. Listen to their suggestions and then focus their attention on the list of suggestions a–j. Ask if any of their suggestions are listed. As a class discuss, which one they think is the best. You could have a vote. Then ask pairs of students to do the same for each of the other problems. Obviously answers will vary, but some like h only apply to number 3 or 16. Discuss the answers as a class and use this as an opportunity to focus on some of the expressions in a–j. For example:
What do you not do to take it easy? (You don't do anything mentally or physically taxing.)

What might it refer to in d? (a terrible headache, really bad toothache)

Where can you have a lie-down? (in bed, on the sofa)

Do you remember 'have a lie-in'?

How can you get some fresh air if you feel car sick or if you're stuck in a room? (open the window)

Ask students if they notice the patterns in the advice and then refer them to the **Real English** note on the use of *Maybe you should* to soften advice. Using *or something* also has a softening effect by giving another unspecified option.

2 What's the matter?

Get students to put the conversations in order and then play the recording so they can check their answers. Play the recording again, pausing after each line so students can repeat, following the same intonation pattern. Then have them practise reading the conversation in pairs. Encourage them to read each sentence to themselves, and then look up and say it aloud to their partner. Point out the collocation *stressful day*. Ask students to suggest what could contribute to a stressful day. Encourage them to record any expressions and collocations from these exercises in their notebooks.

Answers

Conversation 1: 1. c.   2. d.   3. b.   4. f.   5. e.   6. a.
Conversation 2: 1. c.   2. d.   3. f.   4. b.   5. a.   6. e.

3 Further practice

Students should write their conversation and then practice reading it. Have them try to memorise it. You could also get students to change partners and have another conversation. To extend the exercise, write the problems on slips of paper and give one to each student. They should then go around the class, having similar conversations using the problem on their card. When they have finished, they exchange cards and find another person to speak to with a different problem.

4 Health quiz

Check that students understand the expressions highlighted in colour before having them discuss the questions in pairs or small groups. Let students go through the list in pairs, using their dictionaries when necessary Then ask them to memorise three questions and to then close their Coursebooks. Tell them to ask you any of the questions. You should answer their questions. Not only does this give students a model for their own small-group discussion, but it also reinforces the meaning and use of the highlighted expressions.

5 Cures

You could do this as a class discussion, explaining the vocabulary as you go through each problem. Point out the verbs *get rid of, stop, soothe* and *stay*. Ask the class to think of alternative noun phrases that can collocate with each one. For example:
get rid of + dandruff, lice, athlete's foot
stop + a runny nose
soothe + a sore throat, sunburnt skin
stay + healthy, slim

Alternatively, have students discuss the questions in small groups. You may need to explain some expressions in the second task:

- If you have *arthritis*, your joints are swollen and painful.
- *Camomile* is a flower that is used to soothe the skin and make herbal tea.

Listening

1 The NHS

Explain to students that they are going to read about the British health service. Have pairs of students talk about what they know already before having them read the text. By asking them to underline the things that they didn't know already, they are focusing on useful expressions like *some people have to wait over a year before they can have an operation*. Encourage them to record some of these in their notebooks.

For the second task, you should explain that if the government *privatises something*, they sell a state-owned company or organisation and turn it into a private one. Get pairs of students to compare their answers to numbers 1–8 and talk about the questions at the end of the exercise. If you have a story about getting medical attention in a foreign country, tell it to the class. If your students are studying abroad in your country, you might want to take this opportunity to talk about and answer their questions about the medical system. Ask students to read the **Real English** box and model the abbreviations for them. Get the class to repeat each one after you – both as a group and individually. You might need to explain that *the UN is the United Nations, the WHO is the World Health Organisation, the BBC stands for the British Broadcasting Corporation, the EU is the European Union, the US is the United States (of America), the IMF is the International Monetary Fund, UFOs are Unidentified Flying Objects and your CV is your Curriculum Vitae.*

2 | While you listen (At the doctor's)

Introduce the listening task and go over the two questions. Tell students to listen for the answers to the questions. Play the recording, making sure that they cover the text. Get them to discuss the answers in pairs. Tell them to keep the text covered as they do this. They can also share their general reactions to the dialogue.

> **Answers**
>
> 1. Ken had the flu. His mother fell and hurt her back. Later she got a chest infection.
>
> 2. The doctor couldn't see Ken for several days, so he didn't go. For her sore back, the doctor told Ken's mum to go home and lie down for a few days and try to lose some weight. For her chest infection, he told her to take it easy and drink lots of water.

Next, let students read the dialogue as you play the recording again. Then ask students, in pairs, to fill in the first two or three gaps from memory before you play the recording again, this time with pauses so that students can check and fill in the missing words. Do this two or three gaps at a time until the end. Play the recording through one more time with students following the text. If you want students to read the dialogue, or parts of it, in pairs, use the tapescript on page 159. The missing words are highlighted in colour. Encourage students to find any interesting collocations or expressions in the dialogue to ask about and record in their notebooks. Finish up by discussing the questions at the end as a class or in pairs.

> **Answers**
>
> 1. wasn't it
> 2. bad week
> 3. was sweating
> 4. was going to
> 5. appointments
> 6. don't need to
> 7. hardly move
> 8. by herself
> 9. looked her over
> 10. on top of all that
> 11. take it easy
> 12. cutting down on

3 | So what did the doctor say?

As well as some more health vocabulary, this exercise gives students some practice with expressions for reporting advice. Have them do the matching task and then go through the answers. You should point out that *just* in number 1 means *only*. Ask further questions to focus on some of the vocabulary here. For example: *What kind of fluids do you think the doctor means in number 2?*

Can you remember the name of the person who performs operations? (a surgeon)

What kind of ointment could you rub on a rash? (Chamomile is supposed to be good.)

> **Answers**
>
> 1. f.   2. h.   3. a.   4. b.   5. c.   6. i.   7. d.   8. e.
> 9. g.   10. j.

Now get students in pairs to discuss what the problems were. You might want to do the first one together as a class. For example, in number 10, you could be just feeling tired or stressed-out. Pairs of students can then practise the dialogues. Finish up by writing these patterns on the board:

… *(just) told me to + verb*
… *told me I should + verb*
… *gave me … to + verb*

Ask students if they can make some more sentences about other situations with these patterns. For example: *I went and saw my teacher and she told me to keep up the good work.*

Using grammar

1 | Giving advice

Review the expressions for giving advice and write them on the board:
Maybe you should …
Why don't you … ?
You could try … -ing
Have you tried … -ing?
If I were you, I'd …

Remind students that they can soften advice by adding the phrase *or something (like that)*. Explain the task, demonstrate the meaning of *burp*, and then get students in pairs to do the first task. You could then have them change partners for the second part. Encourage them to keep the conversation going. Point out some of the phrasal verbs and prepositional verb expressions:
put (the rent) up
put on (ten kilos)
look in (the chemists)
cut (sugar) out of (your diet)
report (him) to (the council)

Also, ask some follow-up questions. For example:
What are some things the government or the council can put up? (taxes, rent)

What's the opposite of 'put on ten kilos'? (lose ten kilos)
What else could people cut out of their diet? (fatty foods)

2 Should, have to

Students have looked at the difference between *must* and *have to* in previous units. Remind them that *have to* tends to express an external obligation, whereas *must* tends to express a personal obligation. Similarly, in comparison to *have to*, the modal auxiliary *should* reflects a more personal feeling about the advice.

Have students look at the examples and explanation and answer any questions they might have. Then have them apply these guidelines to complete the sentences. They can work individually and then compare their answers in pairs. As you check their answers, ask them to explain their choices. You may need to explain *up front*. If you *pay for something up front*, you pay for it in advance. For example:
You have to pay up front to rent a car in some places.

Point out the common pattern *have to ... first*. Also, encourage students to go back and underline the complete phrases in the exercise and transfer some of them to their notebooks.

Answers

1. have (got) to
2. should
3. have (got) to
4. should
5. have (got) to
6. have (got) to
7. have (got) to
8. have to
9. should

3 *Should* for talking about the future

Should can also be used to express what we expect to happen or to be true. Remind students of the first conditional structure by writing this sentence from Unit 15 on the board:
If they play the way they normally do, they should win.

Again, get students to look at the examples and explanations and answer any questions. Next, have students do the differentiation task. Ask them to explain their choices. You might want to extend the exercise by asking them questions about some of the sentences. For example:

What kind of job is the person applying for? Why do you think he/she wants to have a party if he/she gets it?
What would make you say 'the party should be good'?
What is happening in 2a and 2b?
How could you make lessons more interesting?
What lecture topic would make you say 'that should be nteresting'?

Answers

1a. suggestion
1b. the future
2a. the future
2b. suggestion
3a. suggestion
3b. the future
4a. the future
4b. suggestion

Point out some of the common expressions here for the future use of *should* and encourage the students to record them in their notebooks:
... should be good/interesting
this shouldn't hurt
it shouldn't take that long
I should be finished by nine

4 Matching

This exercise gives students some more common examples of this use of *should*. Have them complete the matching task first and check their answers. Model and practise the pronunciation of the complete phrases, focusing on the way *should/shouldn't* is said. Then have pairs of students test each other, with one person reading the first part and their partner trying to complete it from memory.

Answers

1. f.   2. h.   3. d.   4. a.   5. b.   6. c.   7. e.   8. g.

For the next task have students work in pairs and then practise reading the conversation. You may need to explain that if something has had *rave reviews*, a lot of critics have said it is very good. We can also use the expression *It hasn't had very good reviews*. Point out several collocations and expressions. For example:
I'll have to confirm it with my boss.
I know a good (plumber/dentist/mechanic).
make a really quick/important phone call
Do you think it's worth me ...-ing ... ?
fill in these forms

Also, in the *should* expressions, draw students' attention to the expression *or so*. This makes the number approximate. Ask students some questions to elicit answers with *... or so*. For example:

How much do you pay for a cup of coffee?
How long a break should we have?
How many expressions have you recorded in your notebook today?

Answers

1. There shouldn't be any problem with that.
2. It should be worth seeing.
3. It should be good.
4. It should only cost you ten pounds or so.
5. It should only take me a minute or so.
6. There should be quite a few people there.
7. You should have quite a good chance.
8. They shouldn't take that long.

---

5 | Pronunciation: sentence stress

The pattern practised here is used to say that we don't expect something to be as bad as another person thinks it will be. Have students match the responses to the comments and then play the recording so they can check their answers. Ask what they think is being referred to in number 1 to check they understand the meaning of *cost a fortune*. Point out the expression *well below zero*. Explain that we can use *well* to mean *a lot* in expressions like *well below, well over, well under*. Ask students to guess how many pages there are in their Coursebook using *well over* or *well under*.

Answers
1. b. 2. d. 3. c. 4. a. 5. f. 6. e.

Next, play the recording again and ask students to listen to how *that* is emphasised by the higher pitch. Play the recording one more time, pausing after each dialogue so that students can repeat it. Then have pairs practise it pairs. Encourage the person responding to try saying it from memory.

Follow-up

Have students role-play the conversation between the doctor and Ken's mum, referring to the dialogue on page 141. However, this time the doctor is really helpful and has lots of time to chat. Have students write the dialogue and practise reading it before acting it out for another group. Alternatively, ask students to write a letter of complaint from Ken to the local newspaper about the state of the NHS.

Review: Units 17–20

The exercises here can be used as a test. However, **4 Look back and check** and **8 What can you remember?** are better done as a discussion in pairs.

1 Grammar review

Answers

1. I've known him
2. can't be
3. I used to
4. I never used to
5. I would've come
6. I'd done
7. to take it easy
8. you should go
9. I'll be all right
10. It shouldn't

2 Word order

Answers

1. Do you honestly believe that?
2. Listen, we're obviously never going to agree.
3. Let's just agree to disagree.
4. I just need an aspirin or something.
5. He always wants to know where I am. I hate it.
6. Oh, come on! Just because you're English, it doesn't mean you have to be cold and distant.
7. He can't be more than about twenty-one. He's still in his second year at university.
8. He's a nice guy, but I'd never go out with him.

3 What's the missing word?

Answers

1. a. used   b. ran   c. would   d. as   e. my   f. have
2. a. That   b. was   c. be   d. go   e. as   f. but
3. a. other   b. and   c. fell   d. next   e. had
4. a. who   b. industry c. would   d. who   e. way   f. used
   g. mind   h. Tend

4 Look back and check

Answers will vary.

5 Verb collocations

Answers

1. e.   2. i.   3. a.   4. f.   5. g.   6. j.   7. b.   8. c.
9. d.   10. h.

6 Adjectives

Answers

1. dull   6. commercial
2. nasty   7. two-faced
3. harsh   8. exact
4. Typical!   9. sporty
5. slight   10. snobbish

7 Questions and answers

Answers

1. c.   2. i.   3. h.   4. g.   5. d.   6. b.   7. j.   8. a.
9. e.   10. f.

8 What can you remember?

Answers will vary.

9 Common expressions

Answers

1. lightly   6. eventually
2. ask   7. wrong
3. die   8. not
4. court   9. police
5. sees   10. say

Answers for 11–14 will vary.

10 Revision quiz

Answers

1. *A half-brother* is the son of one of your parents (either your mother or your father). *A stepbrother* is your brother by marriage. For example, if your mother marries another man and that man has a son, the son becomes your stepbrother.

2. A girl.

3. Possible answers: move in together, get married

4. No.

5. You take great care when choosing the clothes you buy and wear.

6. In this day and age, nearly everything: your nose, ears, eyebrow, etc.

7. Possible answers: a marching band, floats, people in costumes

8. No.

9. When you're trying to communicate with someone who doesn't know your language and you don't know theirs.

10. Answers will vary. Yes and no. Stereotypes wouldn't exist if there weren't some truth to them.

11. They damage property.

12. Possible answers: breathe deeply, drink a glass of water

13. Possible answers: They could raid a bank, post office, etc.

14. Possible answers: You could be stabbed, poisoned, shot, strangled, etc.

15. If you had a deep cut.

16. Possible answers: have a filling, have a tooth out, have your teeth polished.

17. Yes.

18. A lotion or cream.

19. Possible answers: a wedding, a birth, a birthday, a promotion, an anniversary, etc.

20. It can be used to describe both. It is fairly common to hear it used for both sexes.